THE SIGN USER'S GUIDE:

A Marketing Aid

Revised Edition

Karen E. Claus, Ph.D.
R. James Claus, Ph.D.

Cincinnati, Ohio, USA

Published in 1978 by The Institute of Signage Research.
Revised edition published in 1988 by ST Publications (Signs of the Times Publishing Co.) 407 Gilbert Avenue, Cincinnati, Ohio 45202 (513) 421-2050

Persons wishing to contact the authors may direct correspondence or inquiries to: Drs. Robert James or Karen E. Claus, P.O. Box 19358, Portland, OR 97219 (503) 293-1610

Printed in Hong Kong by Everbest Printing Co. through Four Colour Imports, Ltd.

Library of Congress Cataloging-in-Publication Data
Claus, Karen E.
      The sign user's guide.

      Includes index.
      1. Signs and signboards—Handbooks, manuals, etc.
2. Advertising, Outdoor—Handbooks, manuals, etc.
I. Claus, R. James. II. Title.
HF5843.C56   1988   659.13'42   88-2019
ISBN 0-911380-83-3

Staff of ST Publications

Publisher	*Jerry R. Swormstedt*
Project Editors	*William H. Dorsey, Erika Golliher, Marti Hinds*
Art Director	*Magno Relojo, Jr.*
Assistant Art Director	*M. Jennifer Meyung*
Production Coordinator	*Carole Singleton Emery*
Typesetting and Paste Up	*Melanie Grace, Judy Robinson, Diana Shelton*

To our family and friends

Contents

Book & Cover Design by Magno Relojo, Jr., Cincinnati, OH.
Cover Photo by Mike Brod, New York, NY

Contrary to the aphorism, Time does not "march on." That is much too bold a concept. No — Time is much too subtle to march, kicking its heels high, in full view for all the world to see. It is far more likely to infiltrate across borders under the dark of night. Then, suddenly, one bright day long after Time has made its entrance, someone looks up and sees Time for what it really is: a sneak.

That is almost the feeling one has when reading the update of Jim and Karen Claus' book: **The Sign User's Guide — A Marketing Aid.** It has been only a decade since the book first appeared in print. But in that short period, things have changed. Not dramatically, not all at once, but gradually, almost imperceptibly, Time has altered the course of the sign industry. This second (and significantly revised) edition of the Clauses' book reflects these changes.

Believe us, there have been a lot of changes. In only 10 years, the industry had undergone what amounted to its own mini-industrial revolution. When the two Phd's returned to the publishing scene to revise this book, they quickly saw an industry in transition. Innovative programs and ideas they had once fought for were now in common use. Computer technology and engineering techniques had begun to transform the sign industry. A major architectural sign design discipline had evolved. The national trade associations, as well as the national trade magazines, had grown tremendously and expanded their horizons.

Perhaps most of all, the Clauses were aware of a new public respect for an industry which 10 years ago suffered from a definite image problem. Whereas the industry then seemed forever at odds with city planners, zoning officials and various other regulatory bodies, much of that antagonism had dissipated. It was almost as if the message which they had preached for over two decades had finally been heard: yes — signs are essential, pervasive elements of the retail sector, the most cost effective form of advertising available to the small business and an important part of the corporate identification program for large businesses.

Supportive statistics and data aside, it was hard for the Clauses to convince members of their "target market," the sign users, that the very success and/or failure of their businesses could dramatically hinge on that innocuous shingle hanging outside their enterprises. Nor was the traditional nuts-and-bolts sign industry ready to accept this concept of product as advertising. In 1978, image and identity and all those words which are difficult to put an exact price on, but which nevertheless have great value, were not thought of in terms of what a sign is, or what a sign does.

Fortunately, businesses are beginning to recognize the economic worth of their signs. **The Sign User's Guide: A Marketing Aid** is no longer ahead of its Time. Its Time is here, today. We hope you appreciate the moment.

— Bill Dorsey
Managing Editor
Signs of the Times

In the decade since the first edition of this book, many changes have occurred in the use and manufacture of signs. When we first coined the word ''signage'' to describe the phenomenon we were studying, the importance of signs to commercial enterprise and land-use planning was not well understood. Since that time, we have seen a transformation occur in the recognition of the importance of this vital communication medium. Though it is still not the subject of careful study by academics, sophisticated planners have come to realize the importance of signage to their communities and have sought to utilize the medium through thoughtful regulation, rather than banish it by harsh restrictions.

In this second edition, we hope to reiterate our intent to provide guidelines that will enable sign users to get the most advertising and commercial effectiveness out of their signage dollars. Since small businesses are more dependent on their signs than any other segment of the business community, we have emphasized this component of the sign-user market. Large corporate enterprises, however, also depend heavily upon the communication functions of signs to enhance their viability. Since signage is important to all forms of commercial enterprise, we have emphasized the economic value of signs throughout the book. We have sought to present a text that is not academic in orientation, but is meant for the sign user.

In revising this user's guide, we are grateful to those who have used the first edition and provided comments. We wish to acknowledge the encouragement and assistance of innovative businessman Noel Yarger. We thank Gordon Keller, president of the World Sign Associates and his organization for their support. We also appreciate John Lamb and Dick King of Cincinnati Sign Supplies who have tirelessly devoted their energy and resources to promoting excellence in the sign industry and expanding the knowledge of the economic and social value of signage. Thanks to our old friend Dennis McLaughlin, attorney-at-law in Spokane, Washington, for always being a willing source of support and information. We would also like to thank Stan Lancaster, Director of Outdoor Advertising, California Dept. of Transportation and Mel Dykeman, Attorney for Outdoor Advertising, California Dept. of Transportation.

We are grateful to Marti Hinds for her editorial assistance. We also appreciate the assistance and additions of the editorial staff at *Signs of the Times,* especially Bill Dorsey. Timely publication would not have been possible without the support and cooperation of Bill Dorsey and the production staff at ST Publications.

— Jim and Karen Claus

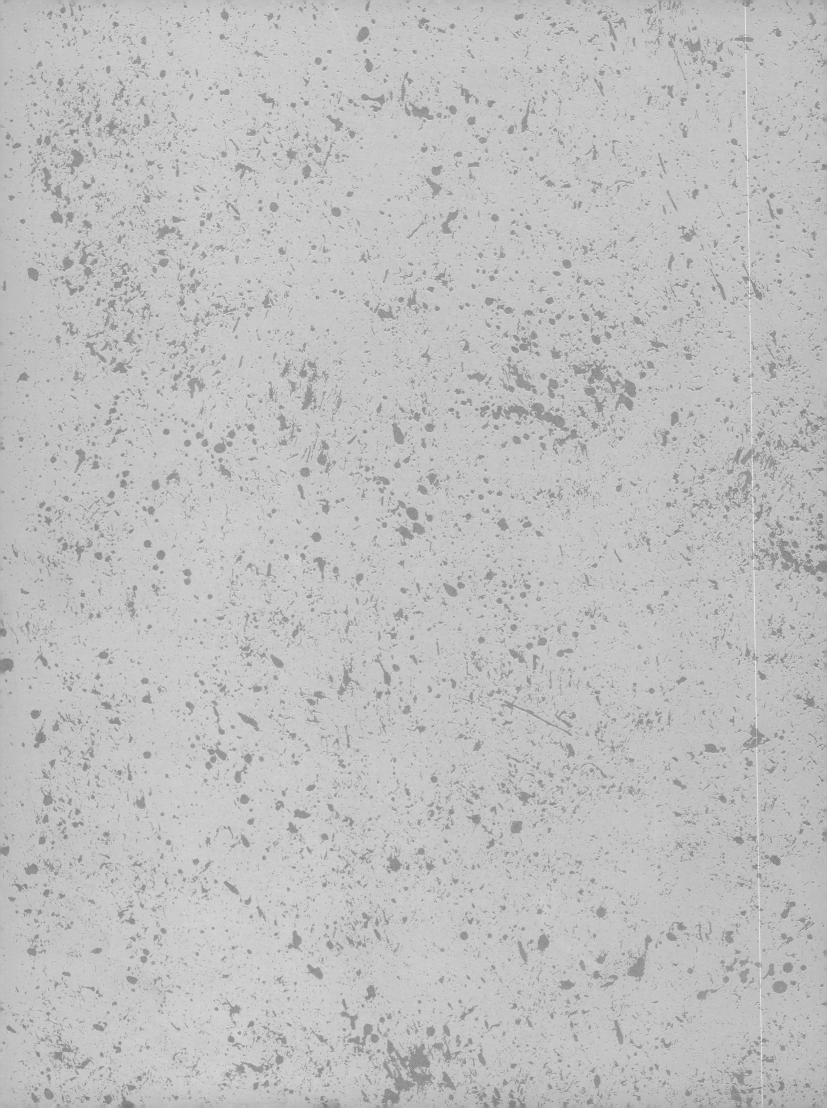

SECTION 1

Fig. 1. Sign identifying

a butcher shop

in Pompeii

*King's Porter
and Dwarf*

Hog in Armour

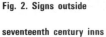

Fig. 2. Signs outside

seventeenth century inns

Bull and Mouth

The Ape

People have long been concerned with how signs look and what they say. Thomas Jefferson was disturbed about some editing changes that the Continental Congress had made in his original draft of the Declaration of Independence. To console him, Benjamin Franklin told Jefferson about a young man, a hatter by trade, who ordered a sign for his place of business. His copy read "John Thompson, hatter, makes and sells hats for ready money." When his neighbors had finished commenting on his choice of words, he ended up changing the copy to "John Thompson," with a picture of a hat.

This story illustrates that signs have an historic tradition which has long been the subject of debate. Everyone fancies himself a sign expert because everyone has made or used signs at one time or another. Indeed, nearly every sighted person in this culture reads and relies upon signs on a daily basis.

The fact that signs have been part of mankind's environment for such a long time can hinder an understanding of the potentials of sign use.

Three important developments enable signs to be used in expanded ways. First, the mobility and urbanity of modern lifestyles demand many ever changing forms of environmental visual communication to serve our more complex cultural needs. Second, space-age technologies provide new design flexibility in the use of materials and in production techniques that would have been unimaginable even a short time ago. Third, scale economies obtained in the mass manufacture of plastics and other materials enable small merchants to obtain signage that would have been beyond their limited budgets just a few decades ago.

Signs Are Landscape Phenomena

Signage, like any other communications medium, functions within a particular setting. In the case of signs, the setting is the landscape. Signs exist in a shared environment — they compete with other media and other signs for the attention of viewers. Unlike most other communication devices, a sign is influenced by its location in relation to buildings, traffic arteries, other rights-of-way and by its proximity to other signs.

As part of the urban landscape, signs are subject to regulation by municipal and federal agencies. Business people need to look at this environment, from the point of view of the planner and the municipal decision maker, to appreciate why some degree of regulation is needed and to see how difficult the task of regulation can be. Similarly, planners must learn to look at signs from the business person's point of view. After you have read this guide, you should be able to express to a planner or other city official why signs are important to your business and why you need to be able to use them with flexibility. A more detailed discussion of sign regulation and legislation is found in the last chapter.

Signs often work best when they are compatible with their environment. Photo courtesy of Colorado Woodsmiths, Inc., Lakewood, CO.

Signs provide such basic information to the traveler that they run the risk of being taken for granted. But what would we do without street signs? Photo courtesy of Gordon Sign Co., Denver, CO.

Signs Help The Traveler

People find themselves most dependent on signs when they are traveling. In an unfamiliar location, we frequently rely on signs to direct us to restaurants, lodging and points of interest. We depend on signs not only to give us direct information — location, the name of the business and perhaps such factors as prices and special features — but also to give us information in less direct ways. From the design and layout of the sign, travelers frequently deduce whether the advertised business will meet their needs. If, for instance, we are looking for a restaurant, we will probably be able to tell from the sign whether the restaurant is quick and inexpensive or if it is more elegant, offering gourmet food.

6

SIGNS HELP COMMUNITIES

Signs And Urban Renewal

Cities are planned in zones. Within each zone, there might be subzones that will not appear on any zoning map but which are obvious to any observer. A central business district may have a "fancy section" or an "ethnic section" or an "historic section." The character of these areas depends to some extent on architecture but is also a direct result of the type of signage being used. From the perspective of the merchant, signs share with architecture an ability to characterize entire sections of a city as well as single establishments. In the Gastown section of Vancouver, BC, a design theme reminiscent of the city's past was enhanced by a signage program that blended with the old buildings. This is highly significant for an economic reason: a sign costs less than a new or remodeled building. And, a new signage program can be an effective substitute for relocation. Compared to signs, buildings are relatively permanent. It is far easier to give a building a new "image" through the use of a sign than through the construction of a new building or even renovation of an existing site.

Sometimes urban changes happen "organically" — through financial pressures, individuals' desires for a different environment, etc. Sometimes however, change is brought about by a deliberate decision on the part of a city government or other political authority. These changes are usually directed by responsible municipal officials, who look at the trends in a city and make deliberate and conscious decisions about which alternative future they would like the city to pursue.

It is interesting to note that signage is the only real mass communication medium that can be of direct aid to the planner in urban renewal. Signs can make certain zones of the city more attractive or give them a particular atmosphere. Urban planners can also use signs to direct consumers and others into the central city.

Signs have the ability to match period architecture. That's one reason why they are so effective in properly conceived urban renewal projects. (See also photo on previous page.) Photos copyrighted by Glen Calvin Moon, 1985, Detroit, MI.

Signs Enhance Mobility

The automobile creates a mobile population. People are able to live and work in two different communities; they take vacation trips by automobile and depend on the automobile for much of their shopping and other errands. This has gradually led certain retailers to modify their market strategy to meet the particular demands of a population in motion. Many businesses have no choice other than to become automobile-oriented. Traffic patterns and street characteristics are prime considerations in deciding where to locate and how to advertise.

Everyday trips are made in patterns. Information of this sort is verified by the work of specialists in the field of traffic engineering. Origin and destination (O & D) studies are used to establish the patterns of movement of persons and goods within an area of interest. A study of this sort can provide an estimate of travel characteristics for an average day. When more comprehensive studies are done, extensive data is gathered, including the purpose of the trip —whether the trip is from work to home or from home to shopping, etc. — as well as social and economic information about the person making the trip. It is not unusual for sign companies to refer to such data when planning the placement of their signs, whether on-premise or off-premise.

Signs enhance mobility — an important consideration when an "emergency" arises. Photo courtesy of Malcolm Grear Designers, Providence, RI. Photograph by Alex Quesada.

Trade Area and Trapping Point

The person traveling from point A to work at point B will want to stop at a gasoline service station (or car wash or corner grocery store or cleaners) that is on the traffic artery connecting point A with point B. Because of this simple fact, the concept of trade area has been formulated. Trade area refers to the district from which an automobile-oriented retailer will draw his customers. In addition, it is known that in any trade area, some points, called "trapping points," have advantages over other locations according to the type of retailing being done. (Claus, R. J., and Hardwick, W. **The Mobile Consumer: Automobile Oriented Retailing and Site Selection.** Don Mills, Ontario: Collier-Macmillan Canada, 1972.)

Signs Improve Marginal Sites

Signs have the ability to keep certain sections of a city from deteriorating in appearance. Several factors explain this. First, all business locations are not equally valuable, and signs can help compensate for locations that have certain disadvantages. In sections of some large cities, it is extremely important to have neighborhood business locations so that local people will be employed near home and have a sense of ownership and belonging in their own neighborhood territory.

Some signs can improve

a marginal site.

Photo courtesy of

Ad Display Systems, Inc., Katy, TX.

A strong nighttime identity

is crucial for round-the-clock

exposure to traffic.

In other cities, changes in the system of traffic routing may cause formerly productive areas to suffer. In these situations, signs can give the appearance and feeling of prosperity at a very low cost. In other situations, traffic may bypass a particular business location, and only its sign enables the business to draw freeway customers. This is not to suggest that only small operations depend on signs in this important capacity. Holiday Inn Corp. reports from research that its sign program is responsible for attracting at least 9% of its customers at each location. An earlier study (Morgan, H. E., **The Industry in the United States: Small Business in Transition.** Tucson, Arizona: The Bureau of Business and Public Research, 1965.) found that on the average, signs attract 40% of the motel business, and in some locations, account for as much as 65%. For a more detailed discussion of motel studies see **Visual Communication Through Signage, Vol. 2: Sign Evaluation** (Claus, K. E. and Claus, R. J. Cincinnati, Ohio: Signs of the Times Publishing Co., 1975.) and the **Appendix of Street Graphics: A Perspective** (Claus, K.E. and Claus, R.J. Cincinnati, Ohio: Signs of the Times Publishing Co., 1975).

In many types of businesses, an on-premise sign can make the critical difference between meeting or not meeting the "break-even point." Because signs are known to increase sales volume, a sign may enable a business at the break-even point to make a profit. (See **Section IV: Street Signage and Business Net Worth Analysis.**)

For many businesses, a sign can effectively increase the trade area through its ability to give a location multiple street frontage. This means that a restaurant with an entrance on one street can "move" to attract customers from the traffic on an adjacent street or highway if a sign is used to communicate with that passing traffic. Restaurants are a good example of businesses for which this extra trade may mean the difference between a profit and breaking even, since the restaurant business has been very sensitive to the impact of inflation and rising food costs. Some businesses have multiple frontage exposure because of their location. Such locations are usually expensive to rent or purchase because of the commercial advantage.

Signs Identify Your Business

Signs also act as identifiers of a place of business. Modern architecture rarely reflects the interior activity. There is a uniformity of architectural style in most business districts that makes it difficult for customers to differentiate shops and businesses by their outward appearance. More often than not, buildings on main streets have changed owners and shopkeepers several times.

The on-premise business sign is the only way a small business owner has of alerting the public that he and his business are located within those walls. Yet even this form of "identification" is a type of advertising. Strictly speaking, probably only public buildings with their names affixed to them have signs that truly "identify" and do little else. (Although it can be argued that an attractive "Public Library" sign is an effective marketing device.)

A business person engaged in manufacturing, retailing or service will need a sign that does more than just "identify." People passing on the street need to be told about the business. Doctors, lawyers and similar professionals do not usually receive business from passersby, although dentists have long used street advertising to attract clients. Appointments and scheduling are important in professional business dealings. So, the small, unobtrusive hand-carved wooden shingle that hangs outside an attorney's office may not be the best sign for a retail business. A small business will probably need to have more than one sign on the premises. In addition to an on-premise business sign, auxiliary signage that informs about specific products or goods, or directs people to park or enter in certain locations may be needed. Again, how these signs are crafted and designed will lend weight to the image that has been created with the main on-premise business sign.

While these various functions of signage can be separated for discussion, they usually act in concert.

Signs can complement

an old building. Photo courtesy of

Amor Sign Studios, Inc., Maintree, MI.

Signs Restore Productivity

It is important to keep commercial buildings productive. The presence of abandoned buildings is a growing problem in many cities. These structures are extremely unattractive, but that is a minor consideration compared to other problems they may create. They invite vandalism, serve as havens for unsavory (and unsafe) characters; increase the cost of neighborhood protection and fire fighting services since arson is a common problem; and do not contribute to the city's tax revenues. If these buildings were kept productive through the use of sign programs, many serious urban problems might be avoided.

The small business person is most concerned with the success of his own business. However, if the businesses around him are failing, he may well find himself in an area which people avoid because of its "blighted" appearance. The business person needs to be concerned with the overall appearance and well-being of his surrounding community.

Signs Attract Newcomers

Americans are mobile, not only in their frequent automobile trips and vacations, but in the frequency with which they relocate their families. Most areas expect a certain percentage of population gain or loss from migrations. In some sections of Los Angeles, for example, many large apartment buildings have a turnover rate that is sometimes as high as 100% annually. This is particularly true in complexes catering to young, single adults.

Population in urban areas is rarely stable. The people present in any city are likely to include many visitors and people who are new to the area. These two important groups need to know what services and facilities are available to them and where they are located.

Signs Help Create Historical and Special Interest Zones

Cities that count on tourism for revenues gain a great deal from the use of signs to enhance special cultural themes (such as Chinatown in San Francisco). Historical motifs are also enhanced by special signage programs. Gastown in Vancouver, or Old Town in San Diego, CA are examples of areas that have used signs to create a theme. Disneyland has also used a signage program to establish historical and fairy tale entertainment themes.

Signs have a special place

in a town's historic district.

Photo courtesy of

Artdev Graphics Corp., Deland, FL.

Signs Can Create Special Moods

Signs today can use special lighting effects to set the particular mood of a place. Cities have successfully used illumination to revive downtown shopping after hours by giving mall areas a feeling of daylight. This specialized use of illumination is rarely discussed in terms of its relation to signs. Since it is gaining recognition as a legitimate part of design, the complementary use of signage should be considered. Dober (Dober, R. P. **Environmental Design.** New York: Van Nostrand Reinhold, 1969, 81-89.) has pointed out that the art of environmental illumination uses the same principles of design as architecture and landscape architecture and is a specialist's field. Illumination is more than canned sunshine and can give the modern pedestrian a unique visual world at night.

In the area of specialty lighting, neon is an excellent medium to create a mood. Photo courtesy of Chris Freeman Designs, Brooklyn, NY.

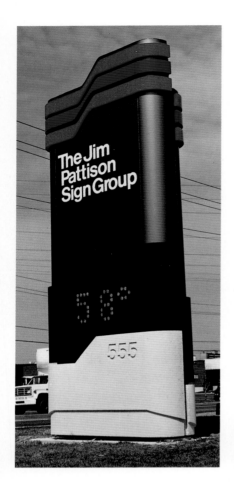

To avoid the problem of habituation, some businesses keep the interest of passersby by incorporating changeable copy on their signs. Photo courtesy of Jim Pattison Sign Co., Scarborough, ON.

A sign can make a city safer by providing additional spill light. Photo courtesy of SmithCraft Mfg., Phoenix, AZ.

Signs Provide Convenience

Signs are also a convenience to inhabitants of a city. Some signs, such as electronic time-and-temperature displays, function primarily as a public service. When the use of these signs (and of all signs) was curtailed in Oregon a few years ago as part of an energy conservation campaign, public reaction to the loss of time-and-temperature displays was immediate and vociferous. People reported that they depended on the signs: some bus drivers said that without the public time-and-temperature displays, it was difficult to keep schedules. Public reaction was so effective that this class of signage was exempted from the ban almost as soon as it went into effect.

Signs Make Cities Safer

During the Oregon sign lighting ban of 1973, another function of signage came to the surface — that of public safety. Police departments have long known that the light from illuminated signs serves to inhibit vandalism and violence on the streets. When the lighting ban was uniformly enforced, increased damage was sustained by shop owners in areas where vandalism had not previously been a problem. Few people will venture forth on dark streets to do quick shopping errands, to window shop, to stop for a snack or even to attend a movie. Few cities can afford to light every step on sidewalks or all of the dark doorways in commercial areas. If a city doesn't want to be dead at night, it must rely upon the illumination of commercial signage, especially if it expects to appeal to residents and visitors who want to "see the sights" and feel safe on the streets at night.

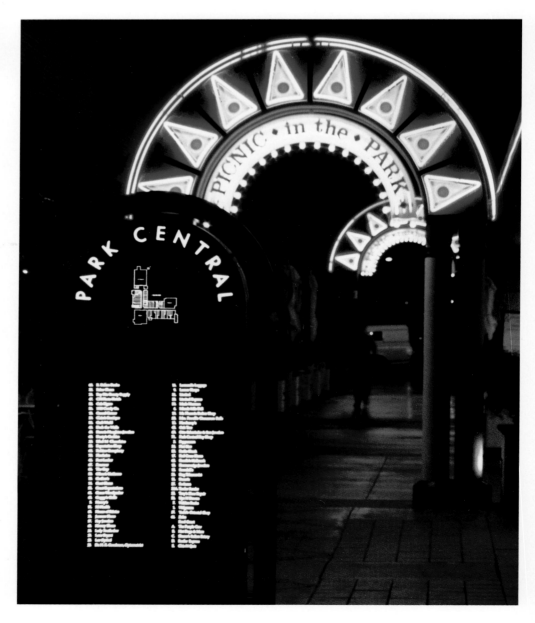

Signs Are An Attraction

No discussion of signs and tourism can neglect the American city where the signs themselves are a tourist attraction. We refer, of course, to Las Vegas, where the signs contribute significantly to the casino atmosphere. Their uniqueness has been a great attraction to people interested in art in the modern environment. (Venturi, R., Brown, D. and Izenour, S. **Learning from Las Vegas**. Cambridge, Massachusetts: MIT Press, 1972.)

Signs Are Image Builders

Visual media, whether pictorial or not, communicate more than the simple content of the pictures or words. Artists who design and produce signs consider many of the same questions as any other artist. The elements that contribute to the message in a painting are also significant in allowing a sign to help project a particular image. These elements may be separated into two categories which partially overlap: 1) physical; and 2) graphic. Sign design is discussed in more detail in Section II.

The physical elements of sign design include considerations such as the size of a sign; its proportion to the building on which it is located; its placement on the building; and its placement in relation to the street. The materials used to construct the sign are also important physical elements and may influence the flexibility of the sign design.

Architectural embellishment is a design function of signage that is strongly related to the materials used to construct the message components. A centuries-old edifice constructed of the most solid materials can be updated to meet modern needs by careful use of the physical elements of sign design. Often, the physical elements of a sign are limited by constraints introduced by a municipal or state legislation. The primary consideration of these controls is intended to be public safety. But some regulations do not work to protect anyone's safety and, ironically, serve as stumbling blocks to competent designers. For example, many codes are based on the assumption that the number of signs or the proportion of sign footage allowed on a building determine the aesthetics of the building. The assumption made is that less is more beautiful.

In many communities, there is an effort to control signs by encouraging "low-profile" signs. This, of course, contributes to an image of subdued taste rather than more traditional advertising graphics, and it is desired by certain kinds of communities. But in order to communicate effectively with passing motorists, a low-profile sign has to be placed close enough to the street to be able to be seen. It is possible to produce a sign that is low to the ground, but no competent designer would choose this style if local setback requirements would not permit the sign to be placed near enough to the street to do its job.

As an image builder, a sign can provide strong, bold identification. Photo courtesy of Creative Signage Systems, College Park, MD.

The graphic elements of sign design allow signs to be flexible in building an "image." These include the use of color; the layout of the copy; the style of lettering; the amount of information; the style of drawing (realistic or stylized); the shape of the message; the use of symbolism; the amount of space; and similar details. Some signs are outstanding in their graphics because they can be read from any angle of approach. Sometimes, however, a sign is difficult to read simply because of its layout. Some styles of lettering are extremely difficult to read on a sign and create a cluttered appearance. The same amount of copy can be made more readable by the astute selection of lettering and the design of the copy-area layout.

The Importance of Materials in Image Design

To some extent, the physical and graphic elements of sign design cannot be separated. The materials selected for use may influence the styles that are possible, or the graphics may dictate that certain materials must be used. Some plastics can be molded so easily that almost any lettering style can be reproduced, although the demands of legibility will not permit many of these avant-garde scripts. New methods are being developed almost daily that allow plastics to be printed using photographic processes so that the images displayed have all the detail and depth of a high quality photographic print.

Modern materials, especially plastics, can be used to create an entirely new image for a merchant. By utilizing modern techniques of sign construction and integrating function and design, it is possible to completely change the visual character of a business. Part II of this book is devoted to a discussion of how to assess a business' needs and how signage helps meet those needs.

22

SECTION 2

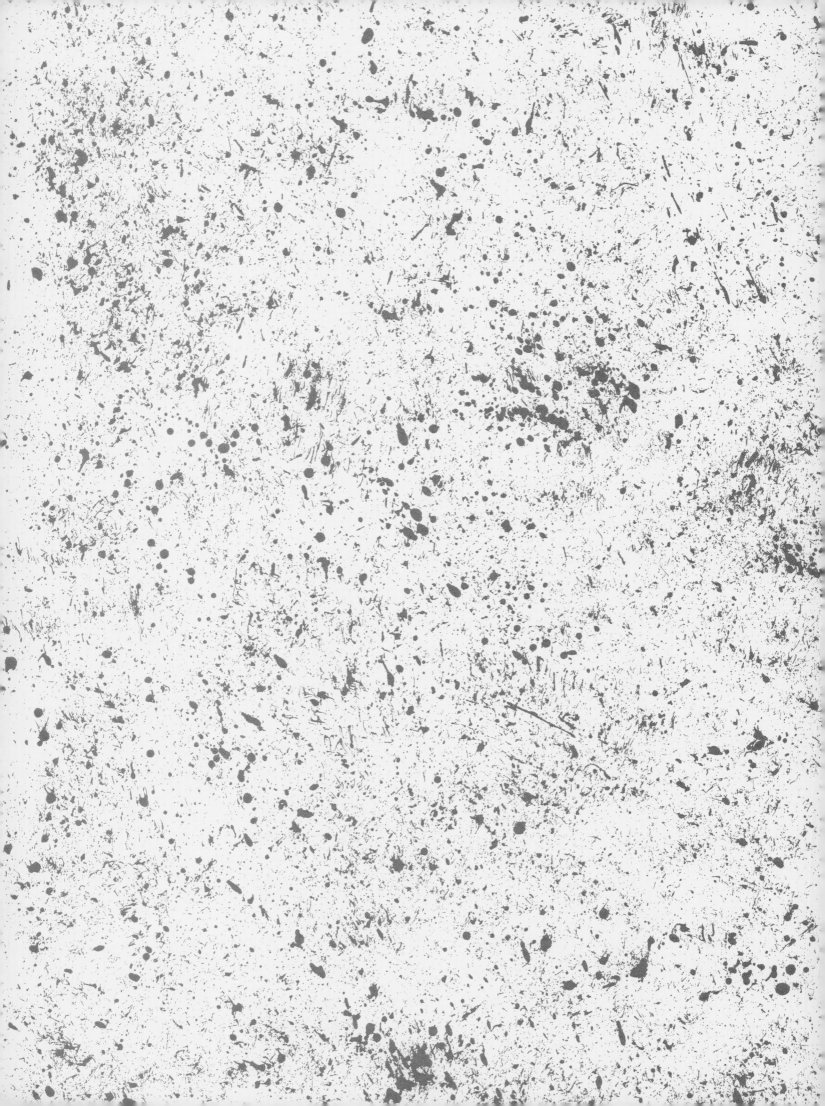

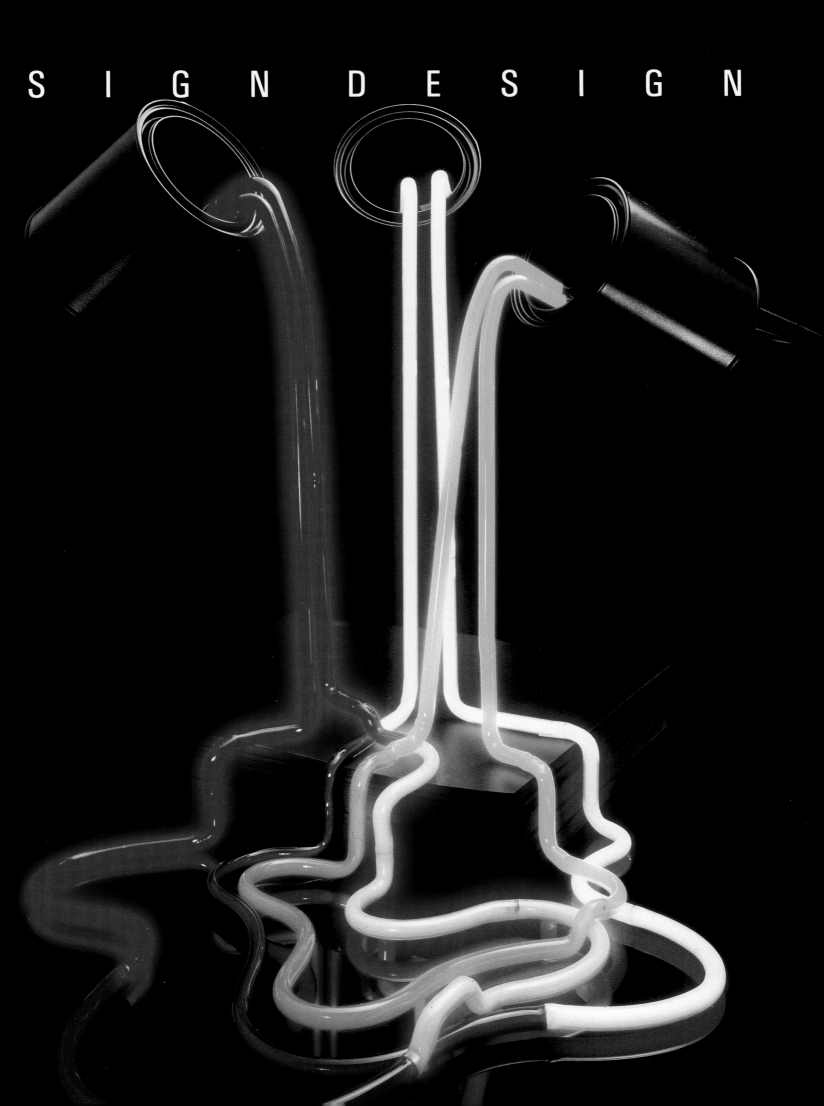

Historic Ghirardelli Square,

San Francisco, CA.

◄

(See photo on previous page.)

Photo courtesy of

Light'n Up Neon, Washington, DC.

THE BUSINESS PERSON CAN CHOOSE AMONG a wide variety of sign structures — roof signs, free-standing signs, projecting signs, wall signs. An understanding of the different types of signs available helps the sign user select the structure which will best serve the needs of his business and reach the most customers. The type of sign selected has a direct impact on the marketing strategy of a business.

The free-standing sign: a monolith rising from the ground. Photo courtesy of Gadsden Signs, Brisbane, Australia.

Types Of Signs

Rather than giving strict definitions of the terms which follow, we will be discussing them generally, emphasizing the different functions which they perform.* (Please bear in mind that while the manner in which we use these words is fairly standard, some local sign codes may attach different definitions to these terms.)

The Free-Standing Sign

A free-standing sign (also called a pole sign or a ground sign) is one which is located on the premises of the business it advertises, but is not actually attached to the building itself. It is supported by one or more columns, uprights or braces in the ground.

* *"A Glossary of Terms Commonly Used in the Sign Industry,"* **Signage Quarterly**, *Vol. 1, No. 3, Institute of Signage Research, gives more exact interpretations of these terms.*

The high-rise sign

attracts customers along

the interstate.

An understated sign is appropriate

for the professional company. Photo

courtesy of Olson Signs & Displays,

Scotia, NY.

Sandblasted brick. Photo courtesy of

G. Ryan Design, Toronto, ON.

The High-Rise Sign

Free-standing signs can be supported by tall poles which enable the sign to be seen from a distance. These are known as "high-rise" signs. Tall free-standing signs offer greater visibility than most other types of signs and are frequently used by businesses such as motels and gasoline service stations. These businesses are automobile-oriented and tend to serve a fairly large number of travelers who may be unfamiliar with the area.

The Low-Profile Sign

Some free-standing signs are built rather close to the ground; these are called low-profile or monument signs. Some people feel that such signs create a more subdued impression than traditional advertising graphics. In addition, these signs often incorporate the support structure into the overall design.

The Wall Sign

A wall sign is a sign which is affixed parallel to the exterior or interior wall of a building and projects less than 18 inches from it. Usually, it has only one face, although occasionally copy is also placed on the sides of the sign cabinet. A wall sign can either be constructed as a box-type sign, with the words attached to a sign cabinet (usually made of plastic); or it can be formed of individual letters which are mounted directly on the wall.

A wall sign is more difficult to read from a passing motor vehicle than is a sign which faces traffic directly. Because of this, the lettering on a wall sign has to be fairly large, and the sign itself usually cannot contain as much copy as a sign which directly faces the street. The advantage of a wall sign is that it can be easily integrated into the overall architecture of the building. Wall signs often function as architectural embellishment.

27

The roof sign offers increased

visibility. Photo courtesy of

Janse Lichtreklame b.v.

Photo courtesy of Douglas Williams,

Woodcarver, Haliewa, HI. Photo

copyrighted 1986 by Keith Karasic,

Kaloa, HI, and the Kauai Eye.

◀

Opposite Page

The marquee sign is most commonly

used by movie theatres. (See photo on

previous page.) Photo courtesy of Ar-

row Sign Div. of White Way Sign Co.,

Chicago, IL.

The Projecting Sign

A projecting sign is a sign which is attached to, and projects from, a structure or building face. It is often perpendicular to the building itself and is almost always double-faced. Because of these factors, it can be read by traffic headed in either direction on a street. Most local sign ordinances limit the size of projecting signs rather strictly, so they tend to be smaller than other types of signs. Projecting signs have long been used in European and older American cities.

The Roof Sign

A roof sign is erected on or above the roof line of a building and is wholly or partially supported by the building. Like a free-standing sign, it is aimed primarily at the distant or motoring public. Studies of the motel industry have shown that, because of the increased visibility which roof signs can offer, they are particularly effective in guiding those unfamiliar with the area to a location.

The Marquee

Marquee signs are signs which form a part of a marquee or canopy. Most commonly used by movie theaters, their large copy area provides room for fairly extensive information. Marquee signs are also used to create an image and often employ spectacular electrical and electronic displays.

The Backlit Awning

The newest entrant — the state of the art in sign design — is the backlit awning. Technically, a backlit awning (also called an electric or illuminated sign) is a piece of reinforced polyvinyl chloride fabric stretched over a canopy-type frame and backlit from the interior by fluorescent or high-output lighting. Because of the high transparency of the fabric as well as its ability to spread light evenly over the entire canopy, a backlit awning provides extremely effective nighttime identification. Meanwhile, the awning portion of the sign provides shelter while the "spill light" brightens dark city streets.

The backlit awning was spawned during the early 80s in the Pacific Northwest — a logical area given its high annual average rainfall. Nevertheless, the trend has quickly spread throughout North America.

As of 1988, several major food franchises have specified backlit awnings for their businesses. The reason is obvious: backlit awnings work. They can provide — in some instances — complete round-the-business identification. In other words, a backlit awning stands out.

No one knows for certain the future of backlit awnings. Right now, they seem to be enjoying a honeymoon of sorts: everyone seems to like them — designers, architects, sign companies, city planners, zoning officials and end users. As they begin to proliferate (as has already happened in some major cities, such as Vancouver, BC), the backlit awning will certainly come under further scrutiny.

Indeed, there are still some major questions which need to be answered. Many sign codes do not presently include backlit awnings in their definitions of what a sign actually is. Similarly, there are technical questions about the engineering of backlit awnings which are just now beginning to surface. Nevertheless, it appears that the backlit awning is gradually becoming a part of the permanent visual environment. Sign users and designers should add this to their list of possible applications.

A backlit awning provides an excellent architectural integration for strip shopping centers. Photo courtesy of K.U. Concepts, Bellingham, WA.

► Minolta's display at
Expo 86, in Vancouver, BC.

▲ Photo courtesy of Fabrilight,
Nashville, TN.

► Photo courtesy of Fabrilight,
Nashville, TN.

► Photo courtesy of
Fabrilight, Nashville, TN.

▲

Photo courtesy of

The Arthur Group, Columbus, OH.

▶

Photo courtesy of Advanced Vinyl,

Bellingham, WA and Cicogna Electric

and Sign Co., Cleveland, OH.

The Awning Sign

An awning sign is a non-illuminated sign which is usually painted or screen printed onto the surface of an awning made of flexible material and which does not extend vertically or horizontally beyond the limits of the awning. Awning signs offer the possibility of three faces for copy. Because they are not illuminated, their effectiveness is curtailed at night; in addition, their limited size means that they cannot always reach potential customers passing by in motor vehicles. The business person should be aware that canvas awning signs require considerable maintenance and lack permanence.

An awning sign offers the possibility of three faces for copy. Photo courtesy of Artdev Graphics Corp., Deland, FL.

The Electronic Message Center

An electronic message center is a sign on which differing copy is shown on the same lampbank, i.e., an electronic or electrically controlled device which displays the time and temperature or other messages. Similar to a readerboard or a window sign, copy can be changed quickly and efficiently. In addition, an electronic message center offers the capability of displaying several messages in sequence. Many businesses use these signs to display public service messages and product advertising.

An electronic message sign not only identifies but also offers the advantage of changeability. Photo courtesy of Ferranti-Packard Ltd., Mississauga, ON.

35

SIGN TYPE RESTRICTIONS

Before selecting the most appropriate type of sign, the business person must consider the regulative and financial restrictions which may limit his options.

Sign Codes

In some cases, municipalities have sign codes which severely restrict certain types of signs. Free-standing signs may be restricted in downtown areas, or roof signs may be allowed only in certain zones or on certain types of businesses. Local sign companies are usually familiar with the legal restrictions on signs, and a copy of the sign ordinance may be obtained from the local planning or building department.

Site

Another factor to be considered before selecting the type of sign used is the business' site or location. For instance, motels or gasoline service stations which rely on drawing motorists from a nearby freeway find it almost essential to use a fairly tall free-standing sign. Because a free-standing sign can be high enough to be visible above the surrounding landscape, and because it can be large enough to be read from a passing motor vehicle, it is effective in reaching mobile consumers who are unfamiliar with the area.

Sometimes a business, particularly a small business, may find itself in a location which has distinct disadvantages. It may be on a less-frequented street where the number of passing motorists and pedestrians is relatively small. In that case, a free-standing or roof sign can act as a location correctional device, enabling customers to locate the store easily. Or it can even give it a multi-street frontage, drawing passersby from several streets.

Not all sites, of course, present disadvantages. Some sites are highly advantageous: the business may be located on a heavily traveled street with a good consumer profile, or it may be at the intersection of two major thoroughfares. A business with a carefully designed commercial communications system will make full use of these advantages.

A business located on a corner should use a sign (or combination of signs) that can be seen from both streets. Similarly, if a business is located on a street that is heavily traveled, perhaps with a great deal of stop-and-go traffic during rush hours, this might be an ideal location for a readerboard. Research studies in perceptual psychology have shown that the eye is drawn to anything new in the environment or landscape. A readerboard, with its copy changed often, can be highly effective on such a street. Not only will the advertising be often seen, reinforcing the message, but a favorable impression of the business can be created, because commuters often appreciate environmental stimuli which relieve the boredom of daily travel past the same locations.

Type Of Business

In choosing a type of sign, the business person should also consider his type of business. A wall sign is often appropriate for a retail outlet that wants to create a tasteful, subdued atmosphere. An electronic message center would not, in most cases, be appropriate for a restaurant that wants to portray an expensive and elegant image to attract an exclusive clientele.

The Needs Of Viewers

Not only should the type of sign be appropriate to the image of the business, it should also meet the needs of viewers. For instance, if a business is tourist-related, such as a motel or some restaurants, it will need a sign that can be read quickly and easily. Often, it will need a sign which can guide people to the business itself. A free-standing or roof sign is usually best for these sorts of situations.

A Shared Environment

By their very nature, signs do not exist in isolation; they are part of a shared visual environment. When considering the type of sign to be used, the surrounding area must also be considered. The most important criterion is that a sign be readable. If one type of sign will be visually blocked by other signs or by other features of the landscape (buildings, trees, etc.), then another type of sign should be considered.

Highway engineers have discovered that along certain stretches of the road, not only does the driver receive a great deal of information, he may also be required to make quite a few decisions (Miller, David B. "Traffic Engineering Principles Applied to On-Premise Signage." Jack E. Leisch and Assoc., Transportation Engineering, Evanston, Illinois, 1977). In situations where this occurs, traffic engineers try to avoid excess information. Similarly, if a sign can be placed so that it is not competing with other information (traffic directions or other on-premise signs), its effectiveness should be increased.

Of course, a business person erecting an on-premise sign does not always have an opportunity to choose where he will locate his sign. But in some cases, careful consideration of the surrounding environment will show, for instance, that a free-standing sign — because it can be some distance from a busy intersection — is preferable to other types of signs.

Frequently, traffic engineers use design models or sketches to plan the placement of signs along a highway. Sketches of the area, including the proposed sign, can be done from the different perspectives that approaching drivers would view the sign. One would then have a good idea of the sign's visibility and would be able to make any necessary changes or modifications before the sign is built.

Signs share in the environment no where better than Las Vegas. Photo by Jim Simon, Santa Monica, CA.

39

Chapter Three

DESIGNING A SIGN

Graphics can be used to emphasize the most important copy elements of a sign as well as to enhance overall design and create a desired business image. Lettering, color, shapes, materials, illustrations and the overall layout combine to make a sign an effective advertising device. (The user who wishes a more complete treatment of sign design is referred to **Visual Communication Through Signage, Vol. 3: Design of the Message,** Claus & Claus, 1976.) Unlike a work of art, which exists in and of itself, things which are designed have a utilitarian function to serve. Tasteful lettering, good color harmony and a beautiful shape will not be effective in sign design unless they present an effective advertising message, creating a sign which is easily readable and which suggests an appropriate image of the business it is advertising.

A sign can "make" the building.

Photo courtesy of CW&H Ltd., Aspen,

CO and Gordon Sign Co., Denver, CO.

Design and Image

Signs advertise in many ways. Sometimes their advertising is very direct and to the point. For instance, a supermarket may have a readerboard that says: "Avocados, 50 cents each." In this case, the advertising is direct, giving concrete information about what products are available and at what price.

Much advertising occurs in far more subtle and less direct ways. Rather than strictly giving concrete information, advertising can create a mood, tell you something about the image of the company and may also convey something about the sorts of products sold. For instance, the sign on a clothing store, through its colors, its choice of lettering and its overall graphic design, conveys valuable and necessary information about the sort of clothing that is available there.

An example of how important sign design can be to a business is the case of a dress shop which offered a wide variety of fairly inexpensive, stylish clothing and catered mainly to teenagers and young women. When a new sign was installed, sales slumped. The new sign conveyed an image of expense and elegance. Those attracted to the store by its sign did not find what they were looking for, and the store's usual customers were turned away, believing that they would not obtain the sorts of clothes they wanted there. (Claus, K.E. and Claus, R.J. **Visual Communication Through Signage, Vol. 3: Design of the Message**. Cincinnati, Ohio: Signs of the Times Publishing Co., 1976.)

When considering the graphics and design elements of a sign, it is very important to consider two factors: 1) who are the customers (or potential customers)? and 2) what is it that attracts them to the store? Sign design should bridge the gap between potential customers and what they want. The sign user must be careful not to let aesthetically sensitive groups pressure him into a design or colors which would not appeal to the target market. Often, local design review committees, composed largely of architects and related groups that service upper income persons, seek to require all merchants to have understated signs that look like those of the more exclusive shops. Unless the business person knows clearly who his customers are and what they want from his store, he cannot effectively demand a design that meets the specific needs of his business.

The independent business person cannot conduct full-scale marketing research to discover who his customers are and where the greatest untapped marketing potential lies. He can, though, talk directly to his customers and get an idea of who wants to shop in his store. This will help him determine what sort of "image" his business should project. More than any other element of the sign, the graphics create the image of a business. Through the use of appropriate colors, shapes and lettering, they give the consumer a "feel" for what the business is like. In many cases, the appropriate image will be what draws customers to the business.

Redundancy and Design

Graphics are also effective in emphasizing a point which the sign user wishes to communicate. Repeating a concept in more than one form makes the message stronger. Redundancy is defined as "giving the same kind of information in more than one way on a given source." (Miller, David B. "Traffic Engineering Principles Applied to On-Premise Signage." Jack E. Leisch and Assoc., Transportation Engineering, Evanston, Illinois, 1977.) Systems developed by traffic engineers use redundancy of design to communicate. An example is the stop sign, where the color red, the octagonal shape and the word "stop" all convey the same information to the driver.

Like highway signs, on-premise business signs need to communicate information within a relatively short amount of time. Redundancy makes the communication more effective and easily understood by the viewer. Designers of on-premise signage often utilize redundancy. For instance, Chinese restaurants often use lettering which looks "Chinese," as well as directly state on their signs that they serve Chinese food. In this way, the viewer receives the sign's information in more than one form. Much of what constitutes good graphics on a sign is this repetition of the sign's message through nonverbal means.

42

LETTERING

Before we discuss the different types of lettering available and the different images which they convey, some basic communication factors need to be mentioned: visibility, noticeability, readability and legibility.

Four Design Criteria for Signs: VRNL

V = Visibility. This is the quality of a letter or number which enables an observer to distinguish it from its surroundings. Other factors which affect visibility are viewing distance and environmental obstructions. (Figure 3 shows standard distance visibility factors.)

FIGURE 3
SIGN VISIBILITY CHART
For 10″ Black Block Letters on White Background

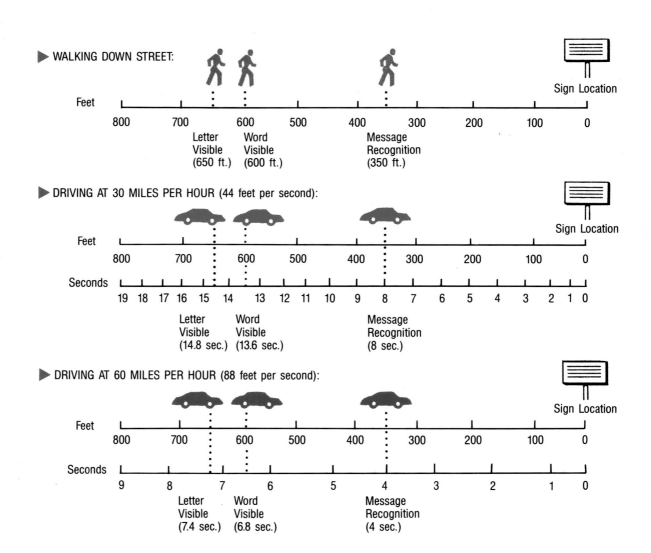

Source: W.S. Meyers and R.T. Anderson, 1974.

Business people should be wary of urban improvement programs which plant certain types of trees in line with store front signs. One community in northern California outlawed overhanging signs and then proceeded to plant bushy privet trees along the sidewalks. These trees very effectively screened the flat fascia signs from the view of all but the pedestrians who were directly in front of a store. This type of "beautification" considerably reduces the trade area of businesses and can lead to the deterioration of shopping areas.

R = Readability. This is the quality which enables the observer to correctly perceive the information content of letters or numbers grouped together in words, sentences or other meaningful forms. For a sign to be effective, it is not necessary that each letter be discernable, but content readability is usually helped by a design that enhances the distinction of each letter.

Readability is a critical factor in encouraging a potential customer to make a purchase decision. A sign message must be readable early enough for a traveling viewer to decide to stop in the vicinity of the store. It is helpful to know the real speed on a street in order to check readability. A merchant can check the readability of his own sign by driving and walking past his store and noting when the sign can first be seen and when the message content is discernable. The speed of travel should be noted, and a stopwatch should be used to determine when the sign first becomes visible and then readable.

N = Noticeability. This refers to the quality of a sign which encourages people to look at it. People usually fail to notice any visual stimulus that is in the environment for an extended period of time. After a sign is up for a while, it will tend to become part of the landscape and will not attract people's attention. This is called habituation. By periodically changing some small element of the sign, such as a design element, or by utilizing a changeable copy part of a sign to display products or special services, a sign can maintain its attention-getting qualities.

L = Legibility. This refers to the characteristics of letters or numbers which make it possible to differentiate them one from the other.

A well-designed sign should score high on all four communication criteria. Since words are the most important elements of sign communication, lettering becomes a critical design factor.

Many signs utilize plain block lettering, which tends to be the easiest to read. However, lettering can do much to enhance the image of the business which the sign presents. The lettering on a sign may suggest that a business is elegant and expensive, or it may suggest discount prices and efficiency.

Today, there is a large variety of lettering styles available. Many type faces, especially those that are ornate, complicated or have very fine strokes, will have to be modified when used on a sign. Changing any letter from a layout board to an environmental display will require some modifications.

The Psychological Connotations of Lettering
Lettering conveys both a message to the viewer as well as certain psychological impressions. A more detailed discussion of this factor is found in **Psychological Considerations Of Lettering For Identification** (Oliphant, Robert, Claus, James and Claus, Karen. Cincinnati, Ohio: 1971).

Slope
Lettering written upwards is usually associated with positive attributes. A downward slope conveys depression and a generally negative feeling.

Slant
Letters that are straight up-and-down or slanted slightly to the right generally do not convey any specific emotion to the viewer. Backward slants are generally perceived to indicate coldness and even calculation; forward slants, on the other hand, tend to be associated with positive emotional attributes. Extreme forward slants, however, may indicate nervousness and an extremely emotional nature. In addition, the combination of different slants within a word or group of words tends to indicate moodiness and possibly unreliability.

Letters that are straight up and down or slanted slightly to the right generally do not convey any specific emotion. Photo courtesy of GNU Group, Sausalito, CA.

Thickness of Letters

Thin lettering tends to indicate simplicity, modesty and refinement. Thicker lettering suggests self-confidence and solidity. In fact, generally speaking, the thicker the letter, the stronger the will or dominance conveyed.

Compression of Letters

Compression refers to the spacing between letters. When a word is highly compressed, it tends to be perceived as indicating clannishness and reserve. Lettering which is extended and large, however, usually indicates a nature which is friendly and open.

The compression of letters often indicates reserve.

Letters widely spaced usually is connoted with friendliness. Photo courtesy of Bloomington Design, Bloomington, IN.

Thick letters suggest self-confidence. Photo courtesy of Art Group, Inc., Pittsburgh, PA.

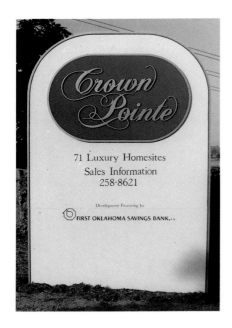

Bold capital letters give the impression of self-respect and pride. Photo courtesy of Oakwood Graphics, Tulsa, OK.

Capital letters which are overly embellished could give the connotation of conceit. Photo courtesy of Uxbridge Carvers, Uxbridge, MA.

Letters which are pointed or triangularly shaped tend to convey energy and quick thinking. Photo courtesy of Ad Art, Inc., Stockton, CA.

Height of Capital Letters

When capital letters are fairly low, almost the size of lower-case letters, they tend to project humility and simplicity. If one wishes to give the impression of self-respect or pride, one should probably make one's capital letters slightly higher than usual. If this is overdone, however, the viewer may receive an impression of conceit.

Shape

Letters which are pointed or triangularly shaped tend to convey an impression of energy and quick thinking; letters which are rounded indicate a more passive and gentle nature. Here again, going too far in either direction may create an impression of, in the case of pointed letters, aggressiveness, or in the case of rounded letters, laziness and indolence.

48

EFFECTIVE SIGN LETTERING

As we have mentioned before, the elements which go into creating a well-lettered sign sometimes differ from the elements which go into lettering used in other contexts.

Spacing

If equal space is given to all letters, the resulting product will not look "right" — it will not have a smooth, professional appearance. The reason is that letters themselves take up differing amounts of space, which needs to be compensated for by changing the amount of space between letters. Leading — the amount of space between the lines of a message — is also important.

Upper- and Lower-Case Lettering

Within the sign industry, there has sometimes been an over-emphasis on upper-case lettering. In fact, recent studies have shown that greater readability and legibility can be achieved through a combination of upper- and lower-case lettering. Part of the reason for this is that a combination of upper- and lower-case lettering most closely resembles the typographical style we are accustomed to reading. In addition, studies have shown that we tend to recognize words more by their size and shape than by individually scanning each letter (Oliphant, Robert, Claus, James and Claus, Karen. **Psychological Considerations of Lettering for Identification**. Cincinnati, Ohio: Signs of the Times Publishing Co., 1971.) Upper-case letters are of a more uniform size, while lower case letters have more distinctly recognizable shapes.

A combination of upper- and lower-case lettering is easy to read. Photo courtesy of The Sign Agency, Euless, TX.

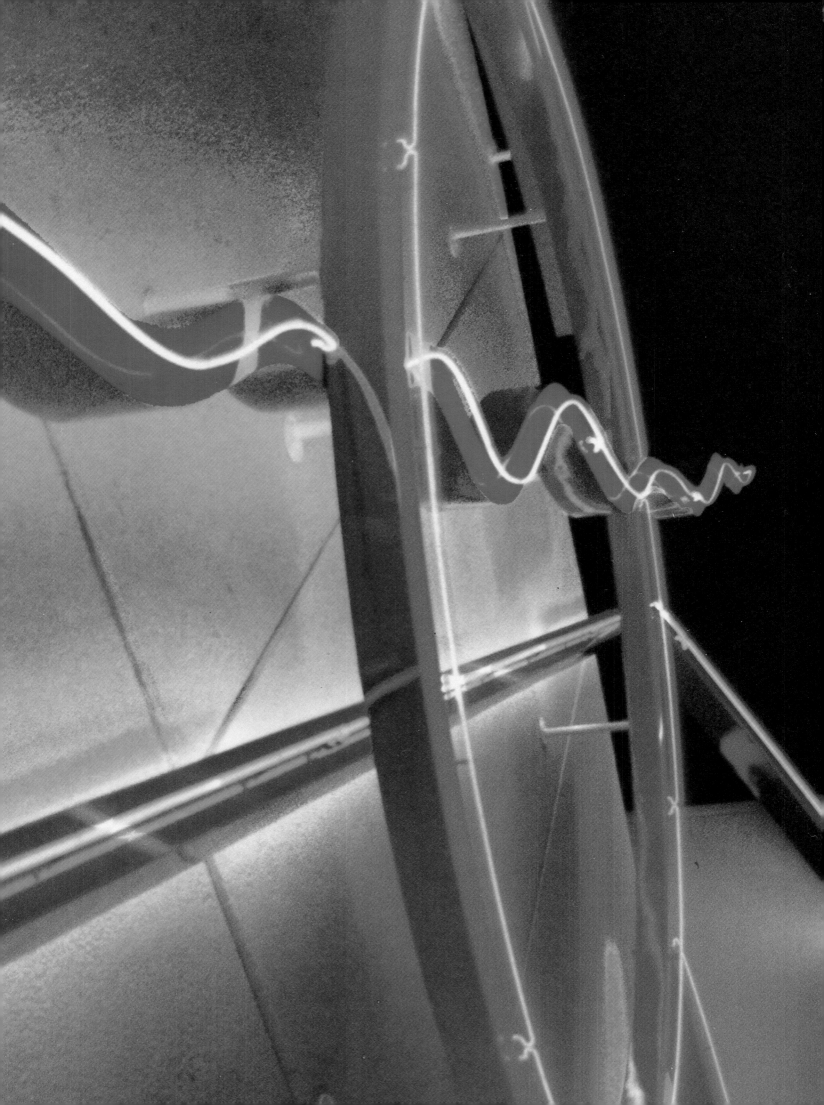

COLOR

It does not need to be emphasized that color has powerful psychological effects. In fact, color is so closely associated with emotion that we use colors when speaking of feelings. We say we "saw red" to describe being angry; that we are "blue" when we are depressed; and we describe a coward as being "yellow."

Color and Visibility

There have been a number of different studies on visibility and color: nearly all of them have concluded that the most important factor in visibility, readability and legibility is contrast between the background color and the color of the lettering. A survey by the Outdoor Advertising Assn. of America, which conducted tests for readability at a distance, ranked color combinations according to their effectiveness. The rankings are listed in Table 1. These findings correlate fairly closely with the results of a number of other studies (Claus, K.E. and Claus, R.J. **Visual Communication Through Signage, Vol. 1: Perception of the Message**. Cincinnati, Ohio: Signs of the Times Publishing Co., 1974.)

An earlier study showed that the combinations of orange on white, red on green, and black on purple were quite illegible and recommended that they not be used (Peterson, D.G., and Tinker, M.A. "How to Make Type Readable." *Harpers,* 1940).

TABLE 1
Best color combinations used in lettering of outdoor advertising displays ranked in order of legibility of letters from a distance

A	1. BLACK on YELLOW		**A**	9. WHITE on BROWN
A	2. BLACK on WHITE		**A**	10. BROWN on YELLOW
A	3. YELLOW on BLACK		**A**	11. BROWN on WHITE
A	4. WHITE on BLUE		**A**	12. YELLOW on BROWN
A	5. YELLOW on BLUE		**A**	13. RED on WHITE
A	6. GREEN on WHITE		**A**	14. YELLOW on RED
A	7. BLUE on YELLOW		**A**	15. RED on YELLOW
A	8. WHITE on GREEN		**A**	16. WHITE on RED

Source: Claus, K.E. and Claus, R.J. Visual Communication Through Signage, Vol. 1: Perception of the Message, Cincinnati, Ohio, Signs of the Times Publishing Co., 1974.

*Atmospheric and ambient light conditions as well as type of letter may affect the legibility of color combinations listed.

Blue's coolness tends to connote dignity, serenity, wisdom and quiet. While its use might not be appropriate for a business which wishes to emphasize speed and efficiency, it might be used by a business which wants to suggest that it has a leisurely pace and a general atmosphere of cultivation and calm. It also tends to suggest stability and is a color often used by banks and large corporations.

Purple has come to be associated with royalty, pomp and luxuriousness. Its visibility factor is low, making it unsuitable for freeway signs, but it is often used for personal service businesses such as beauty salons.

Brown is the color of the earth and tends to connote naturalness and strength. Businesses which want to indicate their strength and mainstream value system often use brown and wood hues in their signs. Brown often connotes ranching and farming. Some fast-food franchises have used brown on their signs to suggest the ranch association of their foods. Brown is basically neutral due to its association with the earth and wood. It is not a color to catch your eye or to suggest action.

White, in Western society, has been the color of innocence. On a sign, it can be used to suggest cleanliness and purity.

Black can be used effectively in signage to create an impression of low-keyed crispness and sedateness. Sophistication also is suggested, if large areas are used.

In assessing these colors, remember that fairly subtle shifts in tint and tone can create large differences in how a color is perceived. While red is appropriate when used in a fairly limited area, when used over too broad an area, it can be overpowering. Similarly, pale yellow can suggest daintiness, whereas a deeper yellow becomes a very sensuous and powerful color.

In choosing the colors to be used on an outdoor sign, the sign designer or advertiser must keep in mind the characteristics of the group toward whom he is directing his advertising. Research has shown that older people tend to prefer blue because it is easier for them to see. Men prefer deep shades of a color, while women prefer more delicate tints. In addition, there is some evidence that people in lower-income brackets prefer bright, undiluted, pure colors, while those in higher-income brackets prefer more subtle shades and tints. Children also react to certain colors positively. Bright colors attract and hold their attention. Yellows and reds are especially attractive to young children. Some fast-food establishments have selected color combinations which appeal to young age groups; for example, McDonald's emphasizes yellow and red.

It is also important to remember that how people feel about a color is very much influenced by the context. When people list their favorite colors, red has a very high rating. But when red is associated with a kitchen, its preference rating drops considerably. Colors of the peach-pink family also receive increased preference ratings when associated with cosmetics, but drop in preference when associated with hardware.

Colors used on illuminated signs are also influenced by the time of day. Many spectacular nighttime displays look poorly constructed or maintained under the harsh light of day. If a 24-hour image is important, attention should be paid to how a sign looks throughout the entire day.

White is the color of innocence. Photo courtesy of Amidon & Co., Sandwich, MA.

Brown, the color of the earth, tends to connote naturalness and strength. Photo courtesy of John Luttman — woodcarver.

The use of an unusual shape may well be worth the added construction expense. Photo courtesy of Art Form, Inc., Van Buren, AR.

SHAPE

One of the first elements of a sign that enters the mind of a passing motorist is shape.

The use of an unusual shape may well be worth the added construction expense. Rohm and Haas' study entitled "Electric Signs: Contributions to the Communication Spectrum" concluded that: "A unique shape appears to be an essential factor in remembering a sign" (Patty, C.R. and Vredenburg, H.L. Rohm and Haas Company, 1970). While the ability to remember a sign has not been correlated with increased sales, it has been found that businesses whose names are remembered by more people have a larger share of the market for their products.

57

Connotations of Shape

Like colors, shapes have certain psychological connotations. A rectangular shape suggests masculinity and solidity while an oval shape is generally perceived to suggest femininity and completion. The shapes of signs (such as those used by American Motors) which are much taller than they are wide give the impression of modernity and forward thinking. A more ornate sign can say something very particular about a business; it can tell the viewer quite a bit about the sort of products that are sold and the overall atmosphere of the shop.

Angular lines and shapes are associated with rising expectations, vigorous growth and activity. Rounded and filigreed designs are associated with calmer, more self-indulgent attitudes. Floral and vine patterns have been found in the artwork of ancient civilizations which had reached their zenith and were experiencing long peace or decline. Analysis of doodles has confirmed some of these generalizations. Men tend to doodle in angular patterns; women tend to draw curvy, flowery patterns.

A computerized animated sequence of neon tubes: an experiment in light from Christian Schiess, San Francisco, CA.

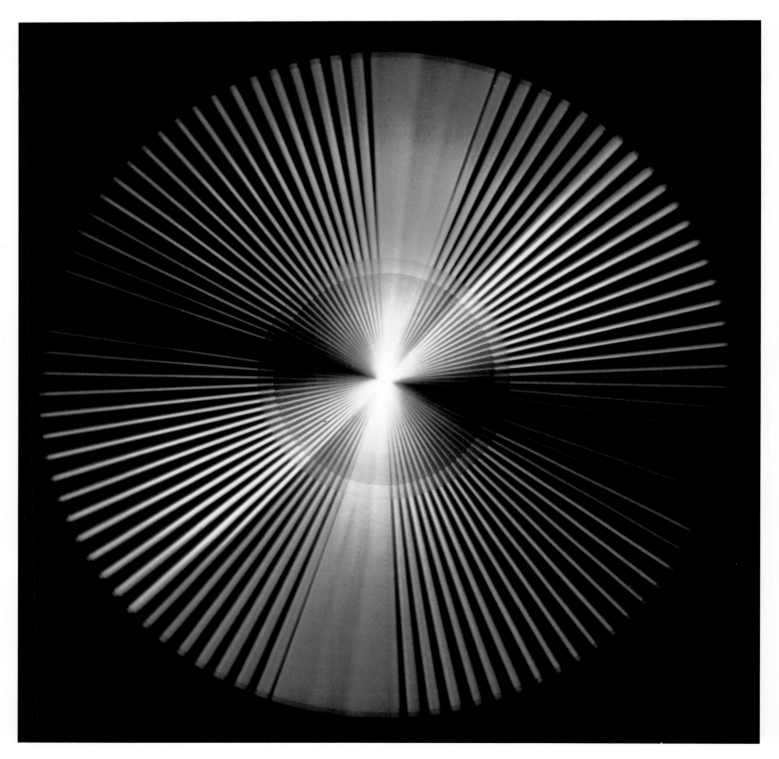

LIGHTING

Lighting enables signs to act as effective advertising in darkness as well as during daylight hours. Almost one-third of all traffic moves at night. The advertiser who wishes to use his sign as effectively as possible should use some form of illumination.

Halation

Halation makes bright areas look larger than they actually are. The greater the viewing distance, the more pronounced the halation effect becomes. A bank of lights, viewed from a distance, will appear as one line. In terms of signage, this means that unless careful attention is paid to irradiation, the words of an illuminated sign, particularly when viewed from a distance, can become illegible.

One-third of all traffic moves at night. Photo courtesy of Creel Morrell Inc., Austin, TX.

Halation makes bright areas look larger than they are. Photo courtesy of Kieffer & Co., Park City, IL.

Floodlit signs are relatively simple — light is projected upon the entire surface of a sign by means of a light source located in front of the sign. The light source is located either above or below the sign and can be either incandescent, fluorescent or high-output mercury. On-premise signs which utilize floodlighting tend to be either painted wall signs or high-rise free-standing signs. The widespread use of floodlighting in very tall free-standing signs is due to the fact that maintenance is much easier when the lamps are accessible from the ground and do not require a service person to go up to the top of a sign in order to replace burnt-out lighting fixtures.

Silhouette signs are illuminated from behind so that the letters stand out darkly against the sign. Typically, they are created by luminous tubing concealed behind opaque letters or behind a valance or cornice. When properly done, these signs can be highly striking. However, great care must be taken so that the effects of irradiation do not make the sign illegible and so that distracting shadows and reflections are avoided.

The widespread use of floodlighting in free-standing signs is due to the fact that maintenance is much easier when lamps are located at ground level. Photo courtesy of James P. Ryan Assoc., Farmington Hills, MI.

Specialty Lighting

In addition to the traditional sign lighting types, there exists a slew of specialty lighting applications which are making inroads in the industry. Some of these types appear to have a "future" in the. . .er. . .future. The following list considers a few of these types.

LEDs, LCDs

The respective acronyms for Light Emitting Diodes and Liquid Crystal Displays, LEDs and LCDs are two forms of lighting which have been extensively used for years in watches, calculators and automobile instrument panels (among other uses). It's only been more recently that LEDs and LCDs have been employed in the sign industry as time-and-temperature units or as some form of electronic attraction panel.

The market potential for this type of lighting is only now beginning to be tapped. Because of a recent technological breakthrough, the LCD's improved brightness makes it a good candidate for exterior signs. LEDs (or solid state lamps) are adequate for most indoor requirements. Both LEDs and LCDs offer the additional appeal of keyboard message programming.

Silhouette signs are illuminated from behind so that the letters stand out darkly against the background. Photo courtesy of Craig Neon, Inc., Tulsa, OK.

MATERIALS

The three primary materials from which signs are constructed today are wood, metals and plastics. Each offers different qualities and design features when used separately or in combination with each other.

Wood

Wooden signs have been growing in popularity largely because of the recent trend toward the "natural" look. Wood signs are probably most effective when used to advertise a business which wishes to emphasize its smallness, or the fact that its products are handcrafted or that it serves natural foods. Wooden signs do present some definite disadvantages. Particularly when displayed outside, they tend to be more vulnerable to the elements than either plastic or metal signs. Unlike plastic signs, they require external illumination. Because of this, they are usually not as effective in drawing customers who are unfamiliar with the area.

The sign user who wishes to take advantage of the look of wood while avoiding its disadvantages can utilize a combination of wood and plastic. Because of the versatility of plastic, a plastic sign can be made which has the appearance of wood, or a sign can have a plastic face and utilize wooden letters or a wooden logo.

Metal

Metal signs can be an asset to a business' image — they suggest high quality, stability and modernity. In addition, because they are so durable, they are well suited to areas where the weather conditions create problems for other kinds of sign materials.

In the 1970s, metal signs were not in widespread use — primarily because of their higher cost and the difficulties of working with the less malleable material. However, in the past decade, the development of an easily machined aluminum composite sheet has changed all this. Today, aluminum foam core signs are quite common — especially for clean, architectural applications.

Wood signs are a "natural" extension of the environment. Photo courtesy of Ireland Peachey & Co., North Vancouver, BC.

▶

Ramada Inn; Opposite Page Since the end of World War II, plastic — as a material — has been a sign industry staple. Photo Courtesy of Architectural Signage and Display, Inc.

▶

The Miriam Hospital; Opposite Page Metal signs suggest high quality, stability and modernity. Photo courtesy of Malcolm Grear Designers, Providence, RI. Photograph by Alex Quesada.

Plastic

Plastic is the material most commonly used for electric signs. Besides the fact that it can be backlit, offering a high degree of visibility and legibility, its single other largest advantage is its versatility. A plastic sign can be made to look like other materials, can utilize almost any type face desired and is available in a wide range of colors.

Vinyl

Slowly, inexorably, vinyl is replacing the most common of all sign substrates: paint. That's because vinyl letters and symbols can be easily drawn and cut by any one of the several computerized sign makers on the market. At the moment, vinyl is being used for virtually all types of signs — both interior and exterior. The days when a sign painter knocked out painted showcards is disappearing. Computers can cut vinyl letters and symbols far faster and more accurately than a sign painter can.

There is still plenty of work for a good sign painter (and probably always be). It's just that the sign painter of the 80s and beyond will have to market his design, layout and craft skills — not merely his mechanical lettering ability.

Porcelain Enamel

This is a material that truly stands the test of time: a porcelain enamel sign almost always lasts longer than the business it identifies. Several generations ago, porcelain enamel was a more popular sign medium than it is today. There are some indications, however, that this trend is reversing as certain business establishments have found porcelain enamel well worth the high price of image.

In addition to these most common materials, the sign user also has available a wide range of other materials.

The human brain seems to respond better to symbols than words. Photo courtesy of Garrity Carved Signs Co., Belmont, MA.

SYMBOLS AND PICTURES

Many on-premise signs utilize some kind of symbol or pictorial directly on the sign. The human brain seems to respond far more immediately to pictures than to written information. We have probably all had the experience of craving a food after seeing it in a magazine or television advertisement. Sign advertising can also use this powerful means of communication.

Changeable Pictorials

The benefits of changeable copy have already been documented. In addition, sign users also have the option of using changeable photographic displays. Mounted on readerboards, photographics are usually used in conjunction with changeable copy. These displays are often used by restaurants to advertise different specials, although they are effective in advertising any product where consumer purchases are influenced by visual stimuli.

The 3M Co. did a study on the effectiveness of these displays in conjunction with Toffenetti's, a restaurant in Chicago which had purchased changeable photographics for its readerboard. Records were kept during a control period and then while the photographic displays were used. From the recorded sales data, it was determined that 96.3% more portions of special feature items were sold when advertised on the photographic sign than when those same items appeared only on the menu. In addition, interviews with customers showed that 78.1% of them saw the sign, and 19% felt that the sign influenced their decision to eat at Toffenetti's (Meyers, Walter S. and Anderson, Raymond T. **The Advertising Media Value of the On-Premise Sign**. National Advertising Company, 1974).

Pictorials can be a powerful form of communication. Photo courtesy of Wood & Wood, Waitsfield, VT.

ARCHITECTURAL HARMONY

Architectural harmony means designing a sign to "fit in" with the overall design of the premises on which it is located. Many people, who are not aware of the functions of signs, assume that if a sign is harmonious with the architecture of the building it refers to, then it is well designed. In fact, some signs blend so well into the overall appearance of the building that they fail to act as effective advertising devices, because they do not catch the attention of the viewer. It has frequently been pointed out that cities thrive on contrast — that is what makes them exciting and vital. In addition, many urban buildings are designed to be occupied by a variety of tenants, and the only way that an individual business can personalize the architecture and make a building — or a portion of the building — distinctive is through the use of unique signage.

This is not to say that architectural harmony is not important. If a business is located in a building which has some architectural distinctiveness, it may well be wise for the sign user to take advantage of this by designing a sign which is integrated into the overall architecture.

In some cases, it is also important to have the sign lettering harmonize with the architecture of the building. This is most important when the lettering is on a wall sign or is applied directly to the building. For instance, a delicate or slanted script on a massive square building, particularly on a lintel, seems to visually weaken the soundness of the structure. Lettering should also serve to embellish and not detract from the overall design of an old building.

69

IntraWest Banks

Photo courtesy of

Adcon, Fort Collins, CO.

Brookview Plaza

Photo courtesy of

Sign Consultants, Inc.,

Minneapolis, MN.

St Louis Union Station

Photo courtesy of

Nordquist Sign Co.,

Minneapolis, MN.

▶

Opposite Page

Photo courtesy of Rosetti Assoc. and

Harv's Neon Service, Inc., Dearborn,

MI. Photograph copyrighted by R.

Greg Hursley, Inc., Austin ,TX.

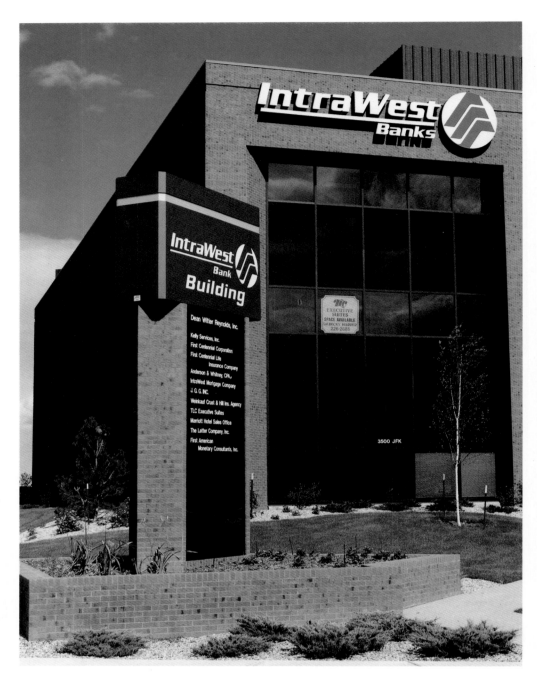

Photo courtesy of

Creel Morrell Inc.

Photo courtesy of

SmithCraft Mfg. Co., Phoenix, AZ.

Photo courtesy of

Valley City Sign Co.,

Comstock Park, MI.

HOW MUCH SHOULD A SIGN COST?

The cost of a sign is important to a small business owner. Several factors should be considered, therefore, when determining how much to pay for an on-premise sign.

A Sign Is An Investment

A sign is one of the most permanent parts of a business and is exposed to weather and constant use. The average life of a sign varies depending on the type of materials used, the construction and other factors. The business owner should find out how many years of service to expect from his sign when he buys it. It pays to purchase good materials if one intends to use the sign over a period of years. A sign in poor repair gives the business a shoddy image.

Maintenance Costs Are Important

Some types of signs are virtually maintenance-free, while others require more attention. Find out, for example, what has to be done to replace a burnt-out bulb or a fluorescent tube. Cheaper materials will often cost more in the long run in terms of repair. No business can afford to have its sign fall into disrepair; a dilapidated sign tells people that the business owner is not concerned with his business' image or its visual environment. Another aspect of maintenance is insurance coverage. It is important to determine who is responsible if the wind blows the sign down and someone is injured.

Maintenance Contracts

The laws regarding mercantile contracts — such as leasing, maintenance and outright purchase agreements — vary from state to state. It is important to have competent legal advice on any contract drafting matters. For the sign user and specifier, the National Electric Sign Association (NESA) recommends that a maintenance agreement should encompass at least:

- A description of the sign, and the location should be clearly defined;
- The monthly payments, deposit and escalator clauses should be specifically outlined;
- There should be an unequivocal "yes" or "no" check which covers all services that are to be extended;
- A vandalism, or an Act of God clause should be included in the agreement. (This protects the sign company.);
- An interest charge for late payment should be added.

Energy Consumption Is Important

New technological developments enable some types of signs to achieve energy savings without sacrificing effect. Be sure to inquire about energy saving bulbs and internal materials when purchasing a sign.

Owning or Leasing

Many sign companies have programs whereby a sign can be leased for a given period of time, and they will maintain it. This may turn out to be a more economical arrangement for a new business, especially if there is any chance that the logo or name may undergo some form of change in the first few years of operation. Statistics show that most small businesses fail somewhere between the first and second year of operation. Perhaps leasing a sign during this period of time would alleviate the requirement for a large expenditure initially, which may be necessary for capital operating expenses.

The National Electric Sign Assn. suggests that all leasing agreements include the following:

- Credit for outage periods should be extended to the end of the lease with no rebate given;
- A provision for the initial payment and the monthly payments to the termination of the lease with no interruption of the payment schedule at the end of the original lease;
- An automatic renewal at 60% of the original rate adjusted for cost of living increases;
- Terms which clearly define liquidated damages if the user cancels the contract.

Some large companies offer standardized types of signs which are cheaper than signs that are custom designed and constructed according to buyer specifications. Many of these standardized units can utilize ingenious design techniques to bring forth creativity and individuality. Often, they can be arranged in different configurations depending on one's needs. Some standardized sign units are nearly maintenance-free and are manufactured with the highest quality materials at a much cheaper rate than similar elements could be if designed from scratch.

How to Choose a Sign Company

In order to choose a sign company, it is necessary to have some understanding of the industry's structure. As is its paradoxical nature, the sign industry suffers somewhat from an identity crisis. Over the course of time, several distinct "personalities" have emerged. The following descriptions capsulize the major components.

The Commercial Sign Shop

The commercial sign industry is made up of the vast majority of small signshops across the US and Canada. These are comprised of the signpainters, the woodcarvers, the pinstripers, the gilders, the calligraphers, et. al. In terms of numbers, this is the largest segment of the sign industry — about 30,000 shops, according to some estimates. Of course, no one knows for certain, because the commercial sign industry is made up not only of a fair number of perfectly reliable and established enterprises, but also includes a number of people who work out of garages, or who hold other full-time jobs, or who don't advertise in the yellow pages, or who make more moves than Mayflower. At present, no reliable demographic information exists which truly tracks this segment of the industry (or defines exactly who belongs to it). To describe the commercial sign industry as "eclectic" would be to understate the adjective.

The Custom Electric On-Premise Industry

This part of the industry — is a group of approximately 3000 to 4000 shops which design, manufacture and install several billion dollars worth of internally illuminated signs per year. The custom electric sign industry truly represents the establishment, and as such, is the best defined in terms of sales volume and demographic make-up. It is also the only on-premise sign industry represented by its own trade association: the National Electric Sign Assn.

The custom electric signshop's genesis dates back to the early 1900s. The introduction of neon in the late 1920s fueled its growth. Luminous tube signs were "custom" one-of-a-kind items in every sense of the word. For that matter, they still are. With the resurgence of neon in the 80s, the industry has continued to thrive.

Production Sign Companies

While custom electric sign companies prosper making individual signs for individual businesses, production or quantity sign companies supply the needs of America's franchises. Essentially a cartel of about a dozen major manufacturers, the production sign company does big business with bigger businesses. Included in this list is literally a Who's Who of Retail America: the oil and automotive companies, the food franchises, the hotel/motel chains, the convenience stores, etc. There are probably not too many towns in this country without a production sign or two. Obviously, the major cities are teeming with countless numbers of these production numbers. And their designs have become highly recognizable symbols along roadside America.

The Architectural Sign Industry

What defines this segment of the industry, and separates it from all the others, is its design function: an architectural sign is an integral part of the environment. Thus, an architectural sign company manufactures a product which both complements and compliments its immediate surroundings. An architectural sign company designs for a structured environment such as a corporate or institutional facility. This is as large a market as it is diverse, and it includes a passel of tenants: airports, zoos, hospitals, office buildings, stadiums, hotels, shopping centers, government buildings, etc. To design for it requires a specialized discipline that is preached and practiced by a group called the Society of Environmental Graphics Designers (SEGD). The several hundred core members of this association are primarily composed of design specifiers who sub-contract the actual fabrication to sign system manufacturers. These firms supply a market which could be described as somewhat of a hybrid of the quantity production and custom sign industries. Translated, that means an architectural sign manufacturer must often provide a large number of signs, but each with its own specific purpose.

Chapter Five

CHOOSING THE COPY FOR A SIGN

The wording chosen for a sign is vitally important. In addition, the number of words used on a sign will directly influence its advertising effectiveness. Perceptual research on how much information the average viewer can comprehend and the practical experience of the sign industry provide guidance to sign users. An understanding of how copy can affect the message is important. The knowledge of certain signage principles, such as the use of keywords and changeable copy, will help the business person increase the effectiveness of his signs.

HOW MUCH INFORMATION SHOULD BE ON A SIGN?

The sign user typically wonders how much information he should put on his sign. Recognizing that his sign is a powerful communications medium, he wants to advertise as extensively as possible without presenting more information than the average person can comprehend.

The Seven Word Rule

The sign industry generally uses the seven-words-per-sign-face rule-of-thumb as a guide. This rough estimate, which came about through the experience of people who design and build signs, is partially supported by the theories and laboratory research of cognitive and perceptual psychologists.

In his classic article, "The Magical Number Seven, Plus or Minus Two: Some Limits on Our Capacities for Processing Information," Dr. George Miller suggests that we process information in "chunks." What constitutes a "chunk" cannot be defined in terms of a definite number of letters or words. It varies according to the previous experience of each viewer (Miller, George A. "The Magical Number Seven, Plus or Minus Two: Some Limits on Our Capacity for Processing Information." *The Psychology Review*, March, 1956).

Different "Chunks" For Different Folks

The same physical stimulus will contain different numbers of chunks for different people (Claus and Claus, 1975). The phrase "Drink CocaCola" may contain a range of chunks depending upon the person viewing the message. The number of letters, syllables or words will not tell how many "chunks" of information this phrase contains. A person who knows the English alphabet, but knows no words of English, would probably treat it as 13 chunks of information. Someone who can read and understand English, but has been completely shielded from advertising, would treat it as three chunks of information. The vast majority of people who have seen this slogan many, many times would be able to comprehend it in its entirety, and would treat it as one chunk of information. Indeed, one of the purposes of advertising is to make certain phrases so familiar that they become instantly recognizable as a single entity.

Approximately Seven "Chunks" On A Sign

In choosing copy for on-premise signage, the sign user should remember that information cannot be reduced to a simple question of "How many words should there be on a sign?"* Seven words is only a rough estimate. Much depends on what those words are and how immediately the viewer will comprehend them.

*One restrictive system used in many local sign codes is based on the simple and erroneous assumption that people can only view seven "items" of information without confusion. The local business person should be on guard against sign codes derived from the model ordinance presented in the book **Street Graphics**. In its original 1971 version, **Street Graphics**, by William Ewald and Daniel Mandelker, proposed a highly restrictive code with severe limitations on copy use.

Some directory signs — even well designed ones — probably have too much copy. Photo courtesy of Roland's Neon Sign Co., Ltd., Windsor, ON.

A more accurate, but more complex, rule-of-thumb would be to use approximately seven chunks of information. A single chunk can be a whole phrase, or it can be a letter. A symbol could be instantly recognizable as a single chunk or could count for several chunks if it contained unfamiliar elements. Some of the factors which will influence the recognizability of sign information are the nature of the market, the visibility of the structure, the marketing strategy of the business and the use of adjunct or media advertising.

Many other factors go into determining how much copy can be perceived by people driving past a particular sign. For instance, if a sign is placed at an angle which makes it more difficult to read, less copy should probably be used. Similarly, if a style of lettering which is not as clear and readable as plain block lettering is used, fewer words may make the sign's message easier to comprehend.

Copy and Type of Business

The information processing capabilities and expectations of potential sign viewers are not the only factors which need to be taken into account in determining the amount of copy on a sign. A careful analysis of the type of business (and its customers and potential customers) needs to be performed. As we mentioned before, a business which is a part of a large corporation that uses media advertising does not need much copy on its sign. The services it provides or the products it sells are generally already recognized. Similarly, certain businesses, such as gasoline service stations or automobile dealerships, are fairly recognizable because of the physical layout of the facilities. These businesses may not need information on their signs that describes the products or services. In these cases, the buildings and appurtenances perform one of the functions usually performed by a sign: the identification of the nature of the business. Even independent gasoline service stations, whose names do not have immediate recognition among consumers, usually do not need to state on their signs that they sell gasoline. That fact is immediately recognizable from the appearance of the site itself. A business which offers a more unusual product or service is a completely different case and may need more copy.

The Large National Chain Store

A store that is part of a national (or regional) chain will often have only the name of the business on the sign. The retail outlets of larger businesses use their signs primarily as identification devices and reinforcement of other types of advertising. Thanks to mass media advertising campaigns, nearly everyone in America knows that McDonald's is a fast-food restaurant which sells hamburgers and that Ford sells cars. McDonald's and Ford no longer have to state the products they sell on their signs, because signs are not their primary form of advertising. Both make extensive and consistent use of other advertising media and are immediately recognized by consumers.

National chains have created such a strong identity that they no longer have to sell products with their signs. Rather, they promote image. Photo courtesy of Oak Leaves Studio.

The Small Independent Business

A small independent retail business needs to communicate with potential customers, not only its name, but also information such as the types of products sold, the prices and the business hours. The sign provides the vital information needed by the consumer. Even if the retailer uses some other form of advertising, such as radio and newspapers, he must still depend extensively on his sign to reach his market.

Sometimes small retail stores expand. When they do, their use of signage changes. As an illustration, we can look at the changes that have taken place over the years on the signs used by the McDonald's system. When McDonald's was a relatively new business without widespread consumer recognition, it used extensive copy on its signs. As McDonald's grew and expanded its advertising budget as well as its recognition among consumers, it placed less and less copy on its signs. The most recent signs contain no information other than the name. The function which had previously been performed by its sign is now being performed by other advertising media.

Copy and Potential Customers

Another factor which needs to be taken into consideration is who the potential customers are. Some businesses rely heavily on customers who return to the store frequently and are usually familiar with the services or products the store provides. Other businesses, such as motels in tourist areas, may be directly advertising to customers who are unfamiliar both with the area and with the business itself. A sign directed toward tourists usually contains more extensive information than one aimed at repeat customers.

Traffic profiles, which are available from city planning or highway departments, give information about the number of vehicles that travel a certain street. In addition, they can often tell what types of "origin-destination" trips occur on the street in front of a business. This information tells whether the street's traffic consists mainly of people traveling to and from work, to and from shopping or for other purposes.

The small independent business needs to communicate with potential customers not only its name, but also such information as products sold, prices, business hours, etc. Photo courtesy of Image National, Boise, ID.

INCREASING THE IMPACT OF SIGN COPY

The use of key words can increase the advertising effectiveness of signs and help establish top-of-the-mind awareness for a business. As discussed earlier, it is wise on most business signs to have one or two key words written in larger type. This is particularly true for businesses which cater to clientele unfamiliar with the area. Words such as "MOTEL" or "RESTAURANT" written in larger letters can cue the motorist who is looking for this type of service. Copy in smaller letters can give more specific details on price, products, services available or any other information the business person believes would be effective in drawing customers to the store.

Consider the one or two words which best describe your business. A clever or strange name will not attract customers unless it has special meaning for them. An unusual name then becomes a tool for market segmentation, because people who do not understand its specialized meaning may not feel inclined to come to your store. People do not tend to be adventurous when considering goods or services. They tend to buy from those businesses they know, have confidence in and feel they understand. It is important for a business to establish some rapport or identification with potential customers. This can be done simply with the proper choice of words for its sign.

Brevity

A sign is meant to convey its message in the environment, amidst a number of competing stimuli. It is, therefore, important for the message to be as brief and readable as possible. A passing motorist should be able to recognize a business as quickly as possible. Short words tend to be more effective than long words; well-known words are more effective than unusual words. It is better to use elements of the sign design to convey an unusual image than it is to play with unusual words.

We have pointed out that signs need to have sufficient information on them. There is also the danger of a sign having too much information. A viewer looking at a sign with too much copy may not only come away with an impression of clutter, he may not even know what product is being advertised. If too much information is given, viewers will "turn off" the communication. The sign user should bear in mind that too much information may end up communicating almost nothing. Often, the cluttered appearance is encouraged by the repeat of information. When a sign says "Restaurant" or "Cafe," it is not necessary to then say "good food." Such duplication can kill the entire message. This is particularly true in automobile-oriented tourist businesses.

A note about symbols is important. Symbols can be helpful or harmful. Be sure that every symbol you select has clear meaning for the customers you wish to reach. Too often, what is thought to be an understandable symbol is only confusing when viewed from the street or in a context that is different from the original symbol's context. People in the environment are usually going someplace in a hurry. You want to catch their attention quickly. An unclear symbol will not get the message across in time for people to make the necessary decisions that will allow them to stop and enter your establishment.

Oftentimes, the size of the sign is directly related to the need for a business to capture the interest of passersby. (See also Quality Inn photo on page 81.)

Kalmia Way

**A reasonably small sign can peaceful-
ly co-exist with the environment. Photo courtesy of Amidon & Co., Sandwich, MA.**

Pioneer Bank

**Middle-sized businesses, such as
banks, usually require moderate-sized
signs which often incorporate time-
and-temperature units. Photo courtesy
of Young Electric Signs, Ogden, UT.**

THE IMPORTANCE OF SIGN SIZE TO ADVERTISING EFFECTIVENESS

In assessing the signage needs of a business and planning ways to design signs which will act as effective advertising, one often has to rely on information that is not scientifically verifiable. Answers to questions such as "Is the lettering of a sign appropriate to the nature of the business?" and "Do the colors of the sign create the desired atmosphere?" are difficult to analyze and interpret using objective methods. But the elements which determine how large a sign needs to be, such as the amount of time the average motorist takes to read a message, the requirements of normal visual acuity and the relationship of these two factors to the speed of traffic on a specific street, can be answered with scientific data.

Few people realize how important the size of a sign is to a business. Merely changing the size of a sign can dramatically alter the amount of business done by a store or other retail outlet.

Sign Size is Related to Business Volume

Radio Shack initiated a marketing experiment to test the effect of increasing the size of the signs on its franchises. The test sample consisted of eight stores, each located in a different state. Dealers selected for participation were classified as having an average or above average volume of business. Prior to the experiment, each test store was identified by either a 3 x 4-ft. double-faced or a 2 x 10-ft. single-faced illuminated sign.

Since the Radio Shack Corp. furnished the sign, and the dealer paid only for installation, it was realized that the gift might encourage a positive attitude in the dealer. So as not to confound the study results, measurement of sales did not begin until two months after sign installation. Inflated purchase figures due to inventory build up were also eliminated.

The sales volume of the eight stores in the test period was compared with the same period a year earlier. Nothing else was done which would have influenced the results of the test, such as extra advertising or special prices. During the three-month test period, the collective sales of the eight stores increased 76.6% over the previous year's purchases. Radio Shack Corp. could not attribute this increase to any factor other than the increased size of the on-premise business signs.

SIGNS AND THE MOTORIST

Almost all signs should be designed so that they can be read from a passing motor vehicle. In nearly every business location, the vast majority of people who see a sign are viewing it from a car or a bus.

HOW WE "SEE"

In order to determine how large a sign needs to be, it is helpful to first understand how the human eye functions and how the brain receives and processes information from the eye. The eye sees, but the brain perceives. This is an important distinction. Not all that enters our visual field is allowed to enter our conscious awareness. Perception is seeing with our mind's eye. A message is perceived as meaningful only when it arouses certain patterns in the brain. Familiar patterns are "encoded" more rapidly than new configurations. Our eye sees many things which are not registered in our mind because the patterns are not meaningful or are considered visual noise.

Contrary to popular belief, it is very difficult, if not impossible, under the normal circumstances of daily activities to "overload" the information processing capacities of the mind. Due to its sensory gauging capabilities, the brain simply will not allow too much information to "blow its circuits." When you are talking to someone on a busy street corner, your brain blocks out the normal street noises. It takes an unusual pattern to catch your attention, such as a loud screech or sudden silence. People who say signs cause information overload and mental stress are not familiar with the functioning of the human eye or brain. This is not to say that there are not certain sets of tasks which may cause high stress due to the requirements of rapid decision-making, such as those confronted by air traffic controllers and intensive care nurses.

The Eye Scans the Environment

Many people assume that the eye functions in much the same way as a camera, taking in static scenes. In fact, if the eye is to be compared to any fabricated instrument, it should be compared to radar. Like radar, it scans the environment, continuously charting what it sees around it. While the analogy with radar is weak and falls apart under serious scrutiny, it is far more appropriate than the notion that the eye is similar to a camera (Johansson, Gunnar. "Visual Motor Perception." *Scientific American*, Vol. 232, No. 6, June 1975).

Normal Visual Acuity

Another key factor to be considered in understanding how the eye perceives information is visual acuity, the sharpness or clarity of normal vision. Dr. Sheldon Weschler, of the School of Optometry at the University of Houston, has studied the subject of visual acuity in reference to signs. Sign visibility is directly related to visual acuity and other principles of vision and suggests that minimal sign standards could be applied to signs, especially those intended to be read by the motoring public. Signs, after all, must be readable by the largest number of viewers possible in order to be effective advertising. Table 2 presents the minimum sizes at which letters can be read at varying distances and by people with different measures of visual acuity. Weschler qualifies the numbers listed in the table with the following statements:

> Snellen letters are most often used as the patterns for visual acuity measurement. The recording method is written as if the measure of visual acuity is a fraction (e.g., 20/20), although that is not the actual case. The upper figure is merely a notation of the distance from the eye to the visual task (the letter). The lower figure represents the size of the visual task. This minor point becomes important in understanding, for instance, that 20/40 visual acuity is not 50% vision but merely a shorthand notation relating to the distance at which a measurement is made (20 feet) and the size of the Snellen letter (.35 inches) that is just recognizable at that distance. . .

The standard visual acuity for a "normal" eye is considered to be 20/20. The standard frequently used as a vision requirement for drivers is 20/40. But the 20/40 standard is a visual acuity level to be attained at the time of licensure. During the four-year period between drivers license visual acuity measurements, the visual acuity of drivers frequently drops to lower levels. For that reason, it may be wise to set signage standards that are based on visual acuities lower than 20/40. (Weschler, unpublished manuscript.)

Visual acuity is usually measured under optimal conditions in a doctor's office, where the viewer is not required to attend to any other tasks. Two important influences, the fact of motion and the influence of color, are not taken into account in tables of normal visual acuity. This implies that the letter sizes suggested by the statistics on visual acuity may not be adequate for a sign in the environment. One other factor needs to be considered: letters on a sign form words, and words are more immediately recognizable than separate, unrelated letters. Words are easier for the brain to process than letters, because they are meaningful chunks of information.

Even if we assume normal visual acuity to be a constant factor, we still must make adjustments for changes in the sign and the angle of the sign in relation to traffic. Roughly speaking, one inch of letter size to 25 feet of viewing distance has been considered about average. No one would argue that the ratios given in Table 2, which describe viewing requirements in a doctor's office, can be directly applied to the motorist attending to the driving task and extracting information from a diverse visual environment. The Table 2 figures are meant to show that there is not a universal norm for visual acuity, and that sign size must be related to the actual visual capacities of the sign viewing public at large.

In highway design, the standard usually used for visual acuity is one inch of letter height to 40 feet of viewing distance. Highway signs have two distinct advantages which on-premise business signs do not have. They are usually directly facing traffic and/or are immediately adjacent to the freeway. In addition, they are almost always easy-to-read white lettering on a green or blue background. Motorists, familiar with the standardized style of lettering and the colors, immediately recognize that they are receiving directional information.

For the on-premise business sign, the situation is usually quite different. Business signs are communicating information which the motorist may not be specifically looking for. In addition, unless the business is part of a national chain, backed up by extensive advertising in other forms of media, the sign itself is not standardized and therefore is not immediately recognizable as offering a certain type of information. When calculating the size of letters necessary for an on-premise sign, therefore, it would be wise to use lower measures of visual acuity.

TABLE 2
Minimum resolvable Snellen letter size of eyes with 20/20, 20/40, and 20/60 visual acuity at distances between 100 feet and ¼ mile

DISTANCE (Feet)	LETTER SIZE MINIMUM RESOLVABLE (inches)		
	20/20	20/40	20/60
100	1.8	3.5	5.2
200	3.5	7.0	10.5
400	7.0	14.0	20.9
600	10.5	21.0	31.4
800	14.0	28.0	41.9
1000	17.5	35.0	52.4
1320	23.1	46.1	69.1

Reaction Distance

Reaction distance is always a complex subject and becomes even more difficult when applied to commercial signage. Reaction distance is a measure of the amount of time it takes a viewer to react to a situation. If a substantial number of people who view a sign are new to a trade area, either as vacationers or business travelers, the amount of time needed to react will probably be greater than that of people familiar with the area. Their reaction distance cannot realistically be compared to the time needed by a local resident who is on the street, say, 30 times a month and who knows the business establishments. The local resident may read only the changeable part or display section of the sign, because the other sections are familiar and have been read many times before.

Any system of measurement has to allow for these differences. It follows that estimates of the necessary or adequate sizes of signs should also include these considerations. The local resident may use the on-premise sign only incidentally and may actually react to a landmark or a configuration of streets in terms of direction. The out-of-towner, by comparison, would rely entirely on the sign. The reaction distance required for each type of viewer, then, is different.

Traffic engineers utilize two types of tables when considering reaction distance. The first lists simple reaction distance and usually includes the time needed for seeing, braking and stopping. The second allows for anticipatory reaction distance. When anticipatory time is added (the time it takes for a person to prepare to stop), more time and distance are needed to react. Tables 3 and 4 illustrate the two types of traffic engineering tables. Designers of highway directional signs know how to utilize this type of information. A standard procedure is to make the keyword larger. Commercial sign designers, on the other hand, have not always understood these requirements. The size of a sign and its elements require balancing between anticipatory and simple reaction distances.

TABLE 3
Simple Reaction Distance

Speed (mph)	Reaction distance (ft.)
30	470
45	700
55	825

Recommended height to distance ratio for letter 1″ to 25 feet. (Optimum viewing conditions)

TABLE 4
Anticipatory Sight Distances
For Standard Traffic Speeds

	Highway Design Speed (mph)					
	30	40	50	60	70	80
Anticipatory sight distance (ft.)	600	800	1100	1500	2000	3000

Source: Miller, David B., "Traffic Engineering Principles Applied to On-Premise Signage," Jack E. Leisch and Associates, Transportation Engineering, Evanston, Illinois, 1977.

Anticipatory Sight Distance

Anticipatory sight distance is a relatively new concept in traffic control. The driver must have time to judge a situation before encountering it and take any necessary precautionary action. This is particularly important at areas of potential hazard and at points requiring complex driver decisions, such as at intersections, interchange exits, lane drops, railroad crossings, drawbridges, toll collection booths, speed reduction zones, etc. In a complex situation, where the driver is presented with difficult choices, ordinary reaction distance may be totally inadequate and unsafe.

The various factors relating to visual perception for operation on a highway, expressed as a sight/distance/speed relation, are shown in Figure 4. The minimum and desirable minimum stopping distances are shown as they relate to the normal range of distances required for driving control. The driver recognizes elements in the visual field which serve as primary cues for the fine control task of his vehicle. Also to be considered is the "focusing distance," the point ahead upon which the driver generally focuses his sight at various speeds. The driver constantly looks beyond the limits of the visual field used for fine control, concentrating toward or beyond his ability to focus. He does so to receive guidance and/or navigational information. Research and physiological studies indicate that this could be on the order of several thousand feet or even more and bears some relationship to anticipatory sight distance. Table 4 gives anticipatory sight distances for different speeds of traffic.

FIGURE 4
Sight-Distance/Speed Relationships

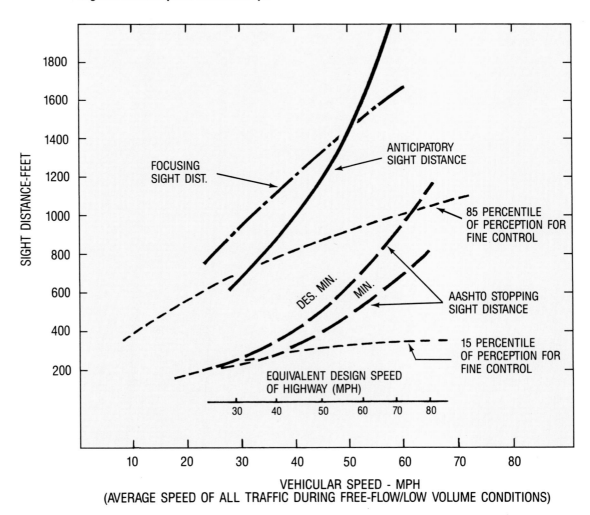

Calculating the Correct Sign Size

It is possible to calculate the optimal size for a free-standing sign if the average speed of traffic on the street is known. We have developed a standard formula, based on reaction distance, which can be used to provide an initial estimate of the minimum size required for the area of a sign.

The Claus Minimum Required Sign Area Formula (MRSA)

A basic formula may be applied to determine the minimum size necessary for safe sign viewing. This formula was developed by R.J. Claus initially to aid planners in determining the average allowable sizes for signs within various commercial zones (Claus, K.E. and Claus, R.J. **Street Graphics: A Perspective**. Cincinnati, Ohio: Signs of the Times Publishing Co., 1975). The formula can aid the sign user in determining the basic minimum requirements for a sign in order to be an effective advertising communication medium. Three important numbers are needed in order to calculate the minimum optimal copy area for a free-standing sign to be viewed by vehicular traffic. These basic figures are:

A = Reaction Distance (simple or anticipatory, depending on characteristics of the site location);

B = Optimal Letter Height (the height-to-distance ratio will change with the letter style and color); and

C = Number of Letters in the Message

Reaction distance tables presented earlier can be used to select the most appropriate estimate. An average figure of seven letters per word can be used if the exact number of letters in the message is unknown.

When the above figures are known, the following formula can be applied: Minimum Required Sign Area (MRSA) = $\dfrac{B^2 C}{144} + \dfrac{.40\ B2^c}{144}$ where: B = Reaction distance in feet divided by viewing distance for one inch of letter height; and C = Number of letters in the message.

Examples

Examples can be calculated using the simple speed/reaction distances listed below. The following calculations will illustrate how the MRSA can be determined for an average city street and for a normal highway.

Sign Size for a City Street

The minimum size for a free-standing sign to be located on an average urban street, using a standard sans serif letter and displaying a message of about 70 letters, is approximately 241 sq. ft. (This is only an approximation used as an example and should not be used as a standard. Each situation requires its own MRSA calculation.) This estimate is derived in the following manner:

1) A = Reaction Distance = 470 ft. at 30 mph
(See Table 3)
2) B = Optimal Letter Height = 18.8 in. (using height-to-distance ratio of one inch to 25 feet; 470 divided by 25 = 18.8 in.)
3) C = Number of Letters in the Message = 70 (10 words x 7 letter average)
4) Copy Area = 18.8 x 18.8 x 70 = 24,740.8 sq. in.
24,740.8 divided by 144 = 171.81 sq. ft.
5) Borders and Margins = 40% of copy area
= 68.72 sq. ft.
6) Minimum Required Sign Area = 171.81 + 68.72
= MRSA = 240.53 sq. ft.

Sign Size for a Highway

The minimum size for a free-standing sign located on a highway, using a standard sans serif letter and displaying a message of 10 words (averaging seven letters per word) is approximately 741 sq. ft. The estimate is calculated in the following way:

1) A = Reaction Distance = 825 ft. at 55 mph

(See Table 5)

2) B = Optimal Letter Height = 33 in. (using height-to-distance ratio of one inch to 25 feet; 825 divided by 25 = 33 in.)

3) C = Number of Letters in Message = 70 (10 words x 7 letters average)

4) Copy Area = 33 x 33 x 70 = 76,280 sq. in.

76,280 divided by 144 = 529.375 sq. ft.

5) Borders and Margins = 40% of copy area = 211.75 sq. ft.

6) Minimum Required Sign Area = 529.375 + 211.75

= MRSA = 741.125 sq. ft.

Measuring the Copy Area

This method is to be properly applied only to the actual copy area of the sign. This is not to be confused with the area of the total structure. In other words, a line drawn around just the minimum area needed for readable copy (including design "white space" for readability) encloses the area we are measuring. This is what is normally regulated in sign codes. Pole covers, supporting structures, embellishments and other features are not part of what we call the copy area of the sign.

Applying the MRSA Formula in the Landscape

Although we present a "formula," it is not meant to be a strict and unvarying means of calculating an ideal sign size for all businesses. Rather, it must be adjusted, taking into consideration the type of sign used, the amount of copy, the type of business, and the lettering, colors and other graphic considerations. Like many models derived from research, this formula usually undergoes some adjustments when it is actually applied in the landscape. It is meant as a guide, not a strict formula.

In some situations, the sign this formula requires might be too large. It might be so big that a municipality's sign code would outlaw it; or it might prove too expensive for a small merchant to erect; or it might be too large for the building.

In cases such as these, modifications can be made. In most instances, not all of the words on a sign are of equal importance. Often, one or more keywords on the sign can be made large enough to be read from the required distance. The passing motorist who is seeking a service is then alerted to the presence of the business and can secondarily attend to the rest of the advertising on the sign, including information about prices and available specials, etc.

The MRSA formula is most useful for businesses which are oriented towards motorists who are unfamiliar with the area and who will be stopping immediately, probably pulling into a parking lot on the premises. While this is true for some businesses, it certainly is not applicable to all commercial establishments. Many types of businesses, particularly those which have a fairly small trade area or are engaged in a relatively rare specialty, do not rely on their signs to draw new customers into their establishment from the street. Rather, their signs act as continued reinforcements, reminding their customers and potential customers that they are there. When customers need the service offered, the sign will have been effective enough as advertising for the customer to recall the business location.

TABLE 5

Actual viewing distances of signs set back 660 feet from road

Distance from perpendicular	Setback	Actual viewing Distance
5,000	660	5,403
4,750	660	4,796
4,500	660	4,548
4,250	660	4,300
4,000	660	4,053
3,750	660	3,807
3,500	660	3,561
3,250	660	3,316
3,000	660	3,073
2,750	660	2,831
2,500	660	2,585
2,250	660	2,344
2,000	660	2,108
1,750	660	1,870
1,500	660	1,638
1,250	660	1,416
1,000	660	1,212
750	660	999
500	660	828
250	660	705
0	660	660

Source: 3M National Advertising Company

FIGURE 5

How to estimate actual viewing distance for setback signs

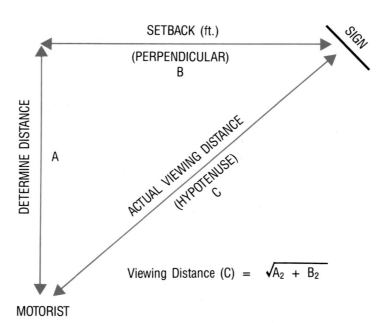

$$\text{Viewing Distance (C)} = \sqrt{A_2 + B_2}$$

This illustration shows how to estimate actual viewing distance between motorist and a sign. The estimator must know the distance of the sign from perpendicular (A) and the setback (E.g. 660 ft.) (B). The actual viewing distance is the hypotenuse of the triangle formed by the perpendicular and the 660 ft. setback (C).

Source: National Advertising Company, 660 Janesville Study, Bedford Park, Illinois, 1966.

SECTION 3

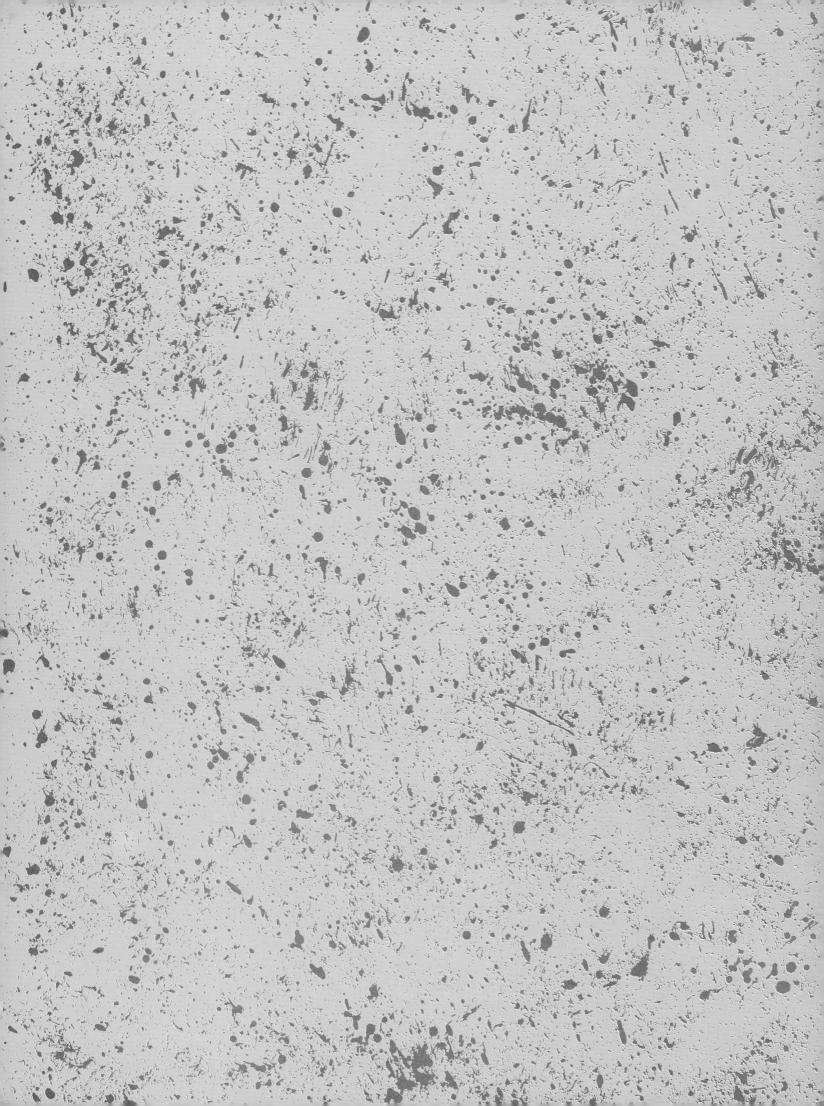

WHY BUSINESSES NEED SIGNAGE

THE IMPORTANCE OF MARKETING

◀

Previous Page

OURS IS NOW A MARKETING ECONOMY, rather than a production economy. In the past, managers focused on the technological aspects of business in order to make gains in productivity. Today's business person must look to marketing in order to increase volume.

Marketing refers to all of the processes and procedures which a business undertakes in order to sell products or services. It includes advertising, as well as product development, pricing, packaging, merchandising and distribution.

THE MARKETING PLAN

The potential-customer profile becomes the basic tool in developing a marketing plan. Signs are an important part of any marketing plan and are the key element in the marketing plan of small businesses.

A marketing plan is a strategic schedule of activities designed to encourage a target group to buy specific goods or services. There are three basic components to any marketing plan: 1) the good or service being sold; 2) the target market; and 3) the communication link between the market and the seller — advertising. Advertising is the central core of any marketing plan.

The Target Market
Markets are people. The mobility of our society today means that many people spend more and more hours away from home. It is, therefore, important for a merchant to be able to reach this mobile market. People who are away from home on a shopping trip, driving to and from work or away on a business or vacation trip cannot be reached by traditional media that are directed toward the home — radio, television, newspapers, mail. Signs are the one medium which can reach a mobile target market most effectively.

Market Analysis
Markets are differentiated by analyzing consumers. There are few products which appeal to everyone living in the marketplace or everyone in the market in transit. Marketing professionals generally try to determine what kind of people buy a particular kind of product or service and then direct their advertising efforts toward those specific kinds of people. This is called market segmentation.

There is more and more emphasis on the analysis of markets in terms of demographics, which simply means determining the distribution of people by types according to education, income, occupation, etc. Since our economy has become so affluent, any given family can buy almost any product or service it wants if it will sacrifice other needs to do so. As a consequence, lifestyle, or psychographic definitions have also become important.

Markets are also analyzed in terms of the attitudes and preferences that actual buyers have at the moment of purchase. Many goods are offered in a way that appeals to impulse purchasers. Food and department store marketing plans might be geared this way.

The mobility of society allows signs to attract more attention than ever before. Photo courtesy of Imperial SignCorp, Port Coquitlam, BC.

◀

Previous Page

A small business has a great need for a sign to market itself with the proper image. Photo courtesy of Great Big Graphics, Hyde Park, VT.

National franchises, such as Safeway, often use signs as marketing cues. Photo courtesy of Ad Art, Inc., Stockton, CA.

Small, independent businesses use "cues" differently than national chains which have supportive advertising. Photo courtesy of Garrity Carved Signs, Belmont, MA.

Signs Are Marketing Devices

Signs do more than advertise, although this is probably their most important marketing function for the small business. Besides identifying a business location, signs can also cue decision-making behavior, target a specific segment of the market and build a business image.

National franchises use signs as cues. In our mass culture, the existence of national franchises influences our economic behavior. At the present time, the fast-food business, characterized by rapid growth and strong advertising efforts, teaches Americans to expect to find the franchises they know when they travel away from home and familiar surroundings. In terms of marketing with signs, this fact implies certain functions. A familiar logo and name on a sign will not have to create an impression for the advertiser and the product. Television and other media will have already done that job. But the sign will perform the important function of providing a cue to the customer who: 1) wants to repeat a particular private economic decision that he has learned from experience; and 2) expects to find the opportunity to repeat the behavior once he sees the cue (the sign) telling him that he has the opportunity. In other words, an advertiser who is well known and is looking for repeat customers needs to use his sign to emphasize his name.

To a great extent, the function of the sign determines its form. The advertiser who knows that his sign must serve primarily as a cue to learned behavior will probably choose a sign that is easily noticed and recognized instantly. The position or placement of such a sign in relation to traffic and street characteristics and in relation to the building it advertises are of paramount importance. Nothing should be done to vary the graphics of the sign from the form that has been made familiar by other forms of advertising.

95

Small businesses can also use signs as cues. Small, independent businesses, whose names are not household words, make up the majority of businesses in this country. To serve their advertising needs, a sign must perform a different function from the "cue" that we have discussed above. The sign may also have to do the job of selling. A person who drives up and down a main street many times a month obviously does not read every sign on every trip. But the signs are noticed, and the information is cognitively stored. When the prospective consumer wants to make a purchase decision, he will use the information that the signs have relayed to him about those main street shops.

In performing its cueing function, the sign message works in an indirect way. The words — the verbal part of the message — may provide information that the customer retrieves from his memory when he finally decides that he should go to a certain store. But the impression of the business created by the non-verbal elements of the sign may do the actual selling. The "look" of a sign, its shape and lettering style, may actually communicate important non-verbal information. Their importance may be equal to that of a well known logo, but for entirely different reasons. Their function is not to act as a reminder, but to create an idea and to build an image.

The dominating presence of a sign can actually become a marketing landmark.

THE VALUE OF ADVERTISING

Advertising builds recognition of a product in a marketplace through reach and frequency.

Advertising can make the difference between the success and the failure of a marketing strategy. Advertising, correctly used, can greatly boost profits.

Many business people fail to take advantage of the relationship between on-premise signage and advertising. Perhaps this is because most of us, including communications specialists, are inclined to think of advertising only in terms of the mass media, such as television and radio, and do not consider that signs also offer a very effective medium for advertising. Advertising is done in myriad ways, and the advertising message can take many forms. Signage is one form. To understand its usefulness as an advertising medium, however, it would be helpful to examine some of the properties of advertising.

What Is Advertising?

At its simplest, advertising can be called a form of commercial communication whose purpose is to persuade a large number of prospective customers on behalf of a product or service. Its specific objective is to be persuasive.

Advertising works in several ways. It builds a memory or awareness of a product or business name and transmits certain information about that product or business. It works to create a favorable attitude about a product or service and builds a particularly enhanced image. Advertising can work to stimulate people to purchase a product or to patronize an establishment. Advertising communicates an awareness of a product and reinforces this awareness by repeating the message over and over again.

97

Two Kinds of Advertising

Almost all advertising can be classified as belonging to one of two broad categories: directional advertising and intrusive advertising. Directional advertising tells people where to buy what it is that they want. This is the kind of advertising people look for when they already intend to make a purchase. You already know what service you need; you merely need information on the specifics.

Intrusive advertising, on the other hand, is information that is provided to the watcher or listener without his specifically looking for it. Advertising on radio and television, for example, is totally intrusive. The broadcast media function primarily as entertainment or as information providers. Airing a commercial message causes a disruption in the normal format. The viewer or listener, willingly or not, must take in the commercial message before the program is resumed. The advertising message provides the viewer or listener with information that he was probably not seeking and tells him about a product or service that he is not likely to buy at the moment the message is transmitted.

The advertisements in magazines and newspapers may be intrusive or directional to varying degrees. Some magazines are read primarily for their advertising content. Most trade journals and even some fashion magazines are read primarily because of the advertisements. Business publications have advertising that is intrusive and directional simultaneously. Most forms of advertising can be a combination of directional or intrusive, depending on the attitudes and needs of the customer at any given moment. For example, a pedestrian walking down Main Street might find the sign in a bakery window to be intrusive if his thoughts are on projects at the office. However, if he is planning to surprise his wife with a special dessert, the window sign displaying today's chocolate mousse cake becomes directional and informative advertising.

Factors Affecting Advertising

Many forces have strongly influenced advertising and have modified it to a great extent. These influences have taken on a variety of forms, but they are essentially of two types: consumer activism and modern technology.

The Rise of Consumerism

In the last decade, we have seen the rise of consumer advocacy groups, that, by organizing in formal ways, have exerted large amounts of pressure on government and business to control advertising. Through lobbying efforts, pocket-book politics and legal challenges, consumer groups have told government and business just what their expectations and needs are. In many cases, this has helped the manufacturer and the distributor of consumer goods.

Consumer activism gives business people an important form of feedback that they were once only able to deduce through indirect means. Consumers want to be given more information about the products and services they buy. They need advertising and have demanded access to consumer information. The US Supreme Court has recognized that to deprive citizens of this essential marketing information is unconstitutional. (*Virginia State Board of Pharmacy v. Virginia Citizens Consumer Council*, 425 U.S. 748(1976).) Consumers' complaints have forced government agencies, such as the Federal Trade Commission and the Food and Drug Administration, to implement regulations that mandate public dissemination of pricing procedures and other marketing information. Defining acceptable television content, unit pricing and food labeling are just a few examples of the changes brought about by consumer groups. These also reflect business' recognition that it is subject to much more scrutiny than in the past, and that the government and the courts will be less hesitant about reacting to consumer charges of wrongdoing.

The Impact of High Technology

An equally influential force acting on advertising today is the impact of advanced technology. The growth of computers — the increasing accessibility of terminals and the flexibility of software — as well as a commensurate decrease in their price have made computers more available for use in all facets of marketing. Econometric computer models have facilitated marketing forecasts and marketing segmentation. Advertisers can now gain a much clearer picture of their markets, who they are, what they are using now, etc. Research on such a sophisticated basis makes it possible to profile reactions to advertising campaigns. This is certainly a far cry from the past when the advertiser could only guess at market penetration and the impact of his product based on whether sales rose or fell.

The introduction of CAD/CAM has raised the industry's high-tech prospects. Photo courtesy of Vomela Specialty Co., St. Paul, MN.

Signs Have Unique Advertising Characteristics

One of the differences between businesses that fail and those that succeed is the extent to which they make themselves known. People are not going to patronize a business unless they have heard of it. Every shop in town cannot, of course, be a household word, but people should at least be aware of a business' existence. By being made aware of what products are sold and where the business is located, they will have added to their choices for making particular buying decisions. The decisions and actions that advertising promotes may be immediate or may be delayed long after the time the customer has seen the advertising.

Signs can sell particular products. Items that people buy frequently in stores are often chosen as an immediate result of advertising. An on-premise sign featuring a sales item will likely cause increases in the sales of that particular item, because people will notice the information on their way into the store. Studies done by the National Advertising Company have reported that on-premise signs contributed directly to the increase in sales of items featured on a sign (Meyers, Walter S. and Anderson, Raymond T. "The Advertising Media Value of the On-Premise Sign." National Advertising Company, 1974). In the case of items that people do not buy often and do not need urgently, there may be a time lag between exposure to the information from the advertising and the decision to buy. If people happen to be satisfied with the product they currently use, they may not be instantly persuaded to try a new product, but may remember the advertisement at some time in the future.

Components of Advertising

Advertising directed toward a target market has two main components: the message and the medium.

The Message

An advertising message consists of the combination of words and images which carries information content to the potential customer. The message must be a link between the products or services offered for sale and the potential customer. To form a strong link, the message must embody aspects of both the item and the buyer. Words and illustrations must both describe the product and appeal to the person who would use that product. An advertising message should be brief and to the point.

The Medium

The advertising message must be carried to the potential customer. Depending upon the customer profile and the size of the target market, different types of advertising media may be used. Some of these media are designed to reach the potential customer in his home, and others are designed to reach him when he is mobile. Signs are effective in reaching a "market in motion."

TYPES OF ADVERTISING MEDIA

There are two basic types of advertising media. They are differentiated by the location of the potential customer when he receives the message. These two broad types of media are "in-home" and " out-of-home."

In-home media appeal to a person who is expected to be — figuratively — in his armchair at home. These media include: newspapers, television, magazines, direct mail and radio.

Out-of-home media expect to reach the prospect who is out of his home. In our mobile society, this could be more hours than he is at home. Prospects who are going shopping or driving back and forth to work or engaging in other social or recreation activities must be reached by out-of-home media. Outdoor advertising, on-premise signage and point-of-purchase advertising displays fall into this category.

In order to evaluate the effectiveness of on-premise business signs, it is important to know how signs compare to other advertising media. Since advertising is such a crucial element in the success of a marketing plan, we are going to give a brief overview of the range of standard media available. Our discussion will focus on elements which are important considerations for the local business person. Large advertisers are already well aware of the attributes of each medium and hire trained specialists to develop complex advertising plans.

It is important to remember that most advertising media are used to reach a specific audience. Advertisers try to determine their primary buying population and then select a media mix and placement schedule to reach the target group. Complete market coverage is generally impractical for most small businesses. Money is wasted when advertising is directed to groups which would not be interested in buying the particular goods or services the business has to offer.

Rate and data materials for media usually include market segmentation information. Studies continually update demographic profiles of the audiences, and rates are established based on the programming attractiveness. Representatives of the media know the make-up of their audiences and can direct advertisers to specific groups. Both radio and television programming make use of a delicate balance calculated to reach certain audiences at specific times of the day. Rates for advertising during the programming are based on the effectiveness of the programming to reach the desired audience.

IN-HOME MEDIA

Television

Television is often considered a national medium because of its capability to reach a nationwide audience. It is extremely effective in advertising brands that have a national or very large market, such as foods, drug products, cosmetics, automobiles and auto-related services and goods. There is no doubt that television is the reigning king of mass media: the average American adult spends approximately six hours per day watching it.

While most small businesses may be out of their league in trying to develop a national advertising program, local use of television can be very effective. Recent trends in television programming, encouraged by an FCC commitment, strike a balance between local and national programming.

The problem with television advertising for small business is cost. There are two considerations: ad placement, buying specific air time for the ad to be shown; and ad production, the cost involved in conceptualizing and producing the ad. While local ad placement is not generally in the thousands-of-dollars-per-spot category, it is still expensive in terms of cost-per-thousand exposures. Repetition is necessary to ensure effectiveness.

Within 48 hours, the majority of people who have watched a television commercial will not be able to recall the message unless they are provided with subsequent reinforcement and reminder advertising. Large corporations long ago realized that signage provides just this kind of reinforcement to national ad campaigns. It is no accident that signs appear in the television commercials of many large companies. When the customers see the sign on the landscape, the commercial message is recalled along with all the other associated images.

Small businesses can take advantage of the expensive television medium if they sell the products shown in national advertising. Point-of-purchase signage is a highly effective way of reminding customers that the products, goods or services they saw advertised on television are available through a particular store or business.

Radio

Radio advertising is often used by small businesses because of its capability to reach specific audiences. A marketing plan should be developed, however, in order to use radio effectively. In a metropolitan market where there may be as many as 10 or 15 major radio stations and another 10 or so that can be "received," the listening audience tends to be fragmented. Even in small cities, local radio stations must compete with powerful stations located in nearby larger cities. The number of persons tuned to a particular station is reduced by all the choices. Radio stations tend to direct their programming to specific target groups in order to capture a particular share of the listening audience. Advertisers must determine which stations best reach their buying public.

Radio advertising is not as costly as television advertising, either for production or placement. An advertiser can place 15, 30 and 60 second spots in various schedules throughout the day: the most costly placement times are commuter hours (7:00—9:00 a.m. and 4:00—6:00 p.m.), when the working public is considered a captive audience. Developing an ad placement schedule for radio requires some foresight on the part of the advertiser. Radio advertising can be sold out weeks in advance. Repetition is crucial for successful advertising: often, for special promotions, an advertiser will place one ad per hour. If several stations are used to provide market coverage, the cost can mount up quickly.

Newspapers

Newspaper advertising is often effectively used by businesses located in small communities. It is generally perceived as local rather than national advertising, although ad campaigns can include many newspapers to give a large market coverage. Newspaper advertising can help a business maintain a favorable image in very small communities since it usually reflects a willingness toward community support and service. Newspaper advertising provides the public with more information than most other media. Written copy allows more specific information to be given since the audience has time to study the message.

Data on newspaper ratings are available through the standard rate and data publications. Before placing an ad, a business person can compare local newspapers with other media available in terms of coverage, frequency and cost-per-thousand exposures as well as reader demographic data.

Magazines

Magazines are often considered a national advertising medium, not economically available to local advertisers. However, the diversity of magazines which appeal to very narrow and special groups can enable local advertising to be cost-effective in certain situations. For instance, if you want to sell a particular tractor to certain kinds of farmers, a magazine can be found which reaches that market. In addition, some national magazines publish regional editions which appeal to local interests.

Another advantage to magazine advertising is that a coupon can be included with the advertisement. This enables the retailer to obtain direct consumer feedback from his advertisement, giving him some of the advantages of direct mail.

Ad schedules are provided by magazines. Circulation figures are also available to the business person who considers placing advertisements in magazines. The advertiser should determine his total market and that it matches the stated market coverage potentials of a particular magazine.

Direct Mail

Direct mail is perhaps the most versatile mass medium. It can be used at any time and can be tailored to the number of recipients. If direct mail is effectively used and blended with other forms of advertising, it can be a very successful marketing tool. The average household receives an enormous amount of mail each week — as many as 15 items per day. At full postage rates, direct mail costs at least 22 cents per mailing. In a market of 15,000 households, this could mean that the postage cost alone is $3300. On top of this cost are the preparation and handling charges.

Direct mail advertising is the most expensive in terms of cost-per-thousand exposures. The expense can be mitigated by the fact that a very timely message can elicit a high percentage of response. Direct mail can be economical for the local business person if care is taken to match the message with the market. Lower mailing rates are available if the advertiser conforms to certain postal regulations, but this may not be of much use to an occasional user like a local retailer.

Directories

Directories, such as the Yellow Pages of the phone book, can be considered an advertising medium, and they are read in the home. They are also a valuable reference. They are informational advertising only; the only exposure occurs when an individual looks for specific information.

OUT-OF-HOME MEDIA

Standardized Outdoor Advertising

Out-of-home mass media advertising is most frequently exemplified by outdoor advertising structures placed along the streets, freeways and highways. These are popularly known as "billboards." Outdoor advertising is done on painted bulletins, large posters or eight-sheet posters and is primarily done on a national or regional basis in larger metropolitan areas. The advertisements and their arrangements are carefully controlled by advertising agencies primarily located in large cities. These advertising agencies conceive the advertising campaign, execute it and deliver it to the public for their clients.

An agency contacts various outdoor advertising companies that have offices throughout metropolitan locations distributed regionally or nationally. These outdoor companies, or off-premise sign companies, own or lease certain pieces of real estate on which they have erected off-premise signage structures. These locations have been thoroughly researched for their ability to deliver a certain amount of advertising to a certain kind of market. These outdoor structures are strategically placed and have particular viewing conditions. Each location is given a rating based on how many cars pass by each day, how many people are in them and what percentage of the market this is.

A local business person can effectively use outdoor advertising to reach a very large percentage of the total market in a month's time. The problem for the smaller business is that it must compete for showing space and scheduling with large national advertisers who are regular clients of the large, distant advertising agencies. There is little chance for local input or control.

Outdoor advertising can be both very cost efficient as well as visually interesting.

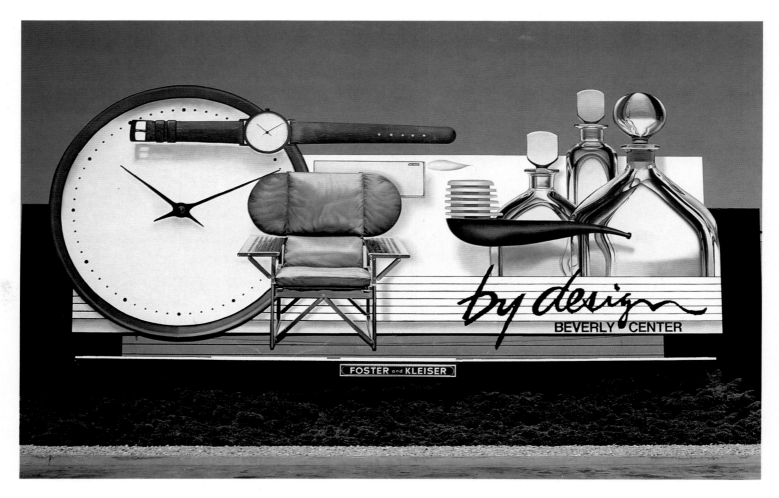

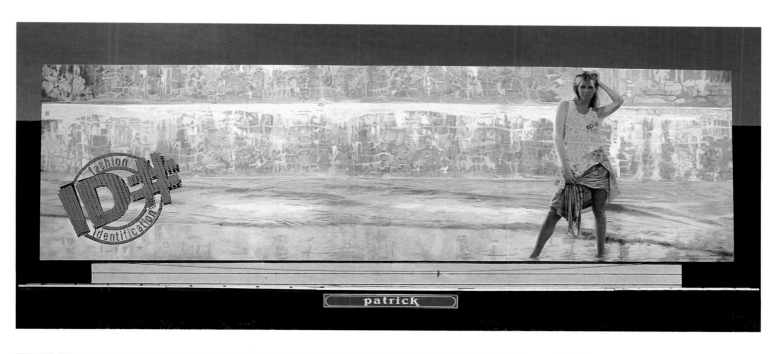

patrick

patrick

patrick

Non-Standardized Outdoor Advertising

Non-standardized outdoor advertising is off-premise signage which is designed to service local areas or specific businesses. Small businesses often use these types of signs, especially in tourist areas. The business person can arrange with a landowner to erect a permanent sign or can contract with a company that owns structures and sells space for given periods of time. Some large national companies provide bulletins for local businesses. These are usually located on heavily traveled highways.

There are two basic ways non-standardized displays are used: 1) In small market areas (under 200,000), these structures are strategically placed to surround a trade area so that a message intercepts people traveling to and from the trade area; and 2) local shopping centers or downtown commercial centers often use the non-standardized billboards to attract shoppers. Another type of non-standardized outdoor advertising which is often seen by travelers is the highway directional sign. This type of off-premise sign directs people to motels, gasoline service stations, restaurants and historical or recreational attractions.

A number of states — to the outdoor advertising industry's chagrin — have instituted a companion program to this type of highway sign. For the record, these "logo" signs (or Tourist Oriented Directionals, as they are called by the Federal Highway Works Administration) are an attempt by the government to control billboards along the interstate. Needless to say, the outdoor advertising industry vigorously opposes the program for a large number of reasons — not the least of which is that the government has no business competing with the private sector.

Indeed, the outdoor industry has been battling with these kinds of environmental issues literally since the turn of the century. Typically, when challenged in court, the industry wins its case on free speech and property rights grounds.

Nevertheless, the continuous fight has led some companies to seek out other forms of out-of-home advertising to get their message to the public. For the advertiser of the 80s, there are many out-of-home alternatives to choose from: bus shelters, transit, fleet marking, park benches, aerial balloons — the list is as long as there is something which can be printed and posted. Of all the forms of non-standardized out-of-home, one deserves more than just a mention: eight-sheet advertisements.

Non-standardized forms of out-of-home advertising include both bus shelter units and fleet graphics — especially effective at night. Photo of Tombstone Pizza courtesy of 3M Advertising Co.

Eight-Sheet Panels

Eight-sheet panels offer the advantages of other systematically planned advertising networks. In function, eight-sheet panels are similar to standardized outdoor advertising, but in form they are a unique medium. A standard billboard ranges in area from 300 to 720 sq. ft. Eight-sheet panels, by comparison, are only 72 sq. ft. in size. In practical terms, this difference is tremendous. A basic advantage of eight-sheet panels over larger boards is that they can fit into places that could not be used by the larger boards. In design, these boards are extremely simple: mounted on one pole, they require very little of a site in terms of space or facilities. They have been used successfully in parking lots and other tight spaces.

Eight-sheet panels are distinct from other outdoor advertising in the great variety of settings into which they fit. Unlike large boards, they are not limited to strictly commercial or industrial areas. These small boards can in fact coexist with other types of activity in a mixed-use area.

The eight-sheet panel is more amenable to local use and control. Local business people may find it easier to schedule a showing in this medium.

On-Premise Signs

As a powerful out-of-home medium, the typical on-premise sign provides great exposure for transmitting a message to the potential market of people passing the front of a retailer's store in cars and on foot. The shopping and driving habits of people residing in a local trading area provide base data for determining the potential reach and frequency of the on-premise sign. (Reach, frequency and cost-per-thousand exposures are standard measures of advertising effectiveness which are used with all advertising media.)

In the study of a typical non-metropolitan county seat having a population of 25,000 and an outer trading zone of 40,000 (for a total of 65,000 people), approximately 85% of these people shopped in the downtown area at least once per month (Meyers, Walter S. and Anderson, Raymond T. "The Advertising Media Value of the On-Premise Sign." National Advertising Company, 1974). In driving down the main street where the retail businesses were located, these same people were exposed to the on-premise signage in front of each retail business.

The study also found that the average resident made 10 shopping trips per month and, therefore, would go by those signs 10 times per month. In advertising terms, on-premise signs on this main street could be said to have reached 85% of the trading area at a frequency of 10 times each month. This reach and frequency was greater than the 65% reach of the local newspaper serving this same trading area. In order to match the sign's frequency of 10 repetitions, the local retail advertiser would have to schedule 10 different advertisements in the local newspaper over a 30-day period. Individual local radio stations rarely exceed 5% exposure to the total trading area market for an average minute of listening. Here again, for the local advertiser to achieve frequency, he must schedule individual announcements several times a week. Direct mail could be used to achieve 85% coverage of this market — but the postage alone for one mailing would be $8287.50. A beautiful on-premise business sign could be purchased outright for the cost of just one mailing.

Similar surveys conducted in urban areas where the trading area is approximately 250,000 people reveals that a typical on-premise sign will have a reach of 40% to 50%, but the frequency remains at 10 per month, as in the non-metropolitan area. While the reach represents a smaller percentage of the total market, the on-premise sign nevertheless is exposed to three or four times more people because of the much greater population of the trading area. The comparison to other media choices in the urban area is even more favorable for the on-premise sign. An individual retailer in a large metropolitan market can effectively serve only 10% to 20% of that market. If he elects to use newspaper, radio or television, he is forced to buy an enormous amount of non-usable circulation. That usually means that his true cost-per-thousand exposures of reaching people who can buy from his location can be in the range of $10 to $20 per thousand.

The on-premise sign is very economical in terms of cost-per-thousand exposures. Variables affecting the cost of on-premise sign advertising depend on the amount of traffic going by the location, the cost of the sign itself and the amortization practice of the sign owner. (Amortization refers to the economic life of a sign or sign face. Frequently, regulators use amortization as a form of compensation for a taking. The sign is allowed to remain for a limited time period rather than be removed and require monetary compensation.) For an average case in a non-metropolitan market where the main street traffic is at least 15,000 vehicles per day (and assuming a very short amortization period of five years), the cost-per-thousand exposures is around six cents. The on-premise sign in the urban area, where arterial street traffic is in the range of 30,000 vehicles per day or greater, means three cents per thousand for the same kind of sign. So, the on-premise sign, considered as an advertising medium, not only delivers a high degree of reach and frequency (usually greater than other local media), but it does this for pennies per thousand compared to dollars per thousand for other media.

Advertising media must do more than deliver a high degree of reach and frequency at low cost per thousand. The advertising message must penetrate the minds of those exposed to the message. The message must be read, remembered and acted upon. Surveys conducted by the 3M Co. in conjunction with sign owners, have sought to obtain data on awareness. Three such studies have focused on restaurants. One study was in conjunction with Denny's restaurants in Los Angeles; another with Toffenetti's in downtown Chicago; and a third, with a Ramada Inn location in Burr Ridge, IL. Almost 4000 personal interviews were conducted to determine customer reaction to the advertising messages which appeared on the copy boards of the on-premise signs. In each case, the copy was changed daily to advertise a special. The special also indicated the price. Readership scores ranged from 61% where letters alone were used to 78% where changeable letters and changeable pictorials were used.

The key question is "Did these advertising messages attract more people to the restaurant than would normally have come?" According to their responses, 13% more people came to the Ramada restaurant as a result of reading the sign message; 15% more for Denny's; and 20% more for Toffenetti's.

Point-of-Purchase Advertising Displays
Point-of-purchase displays are a form of out-of-home advertising which appeals to the "impulse" tendencies of shoppers to purchase smaller goods which are secondary to their primary needs. This type of signage is seen in supermarkets, drugstores, discount department stores and auto service stations. Point-of-purchase displays are designed to appeal to particular market segments. For example, certain candy products are placed strategically throughout supermarkets at the eye level of children between the ages of six and 10. These placements are well researched and may even be required in marketing agreements between product manufacturers and supermarkets.

The Concept of Media Mix
If possible, a local advertiser should use a combination of media. If a retailer has weekly promotions and a substantial number of items and products to be included in a weekly special, then he obviously must use the local newspaper. Typical of this would be the weekly supermarket advertisements.

In an advertiser's media mix, funds to support an on-premise sign program should be included. Signs can be important devices to reinforce ads that appear in other media. On-premise sign advertising can be coordinated with newspaper and local radio advertising. The same message can be displayed in a number of media. Direct mail will be more effective if it is combined with the on-premise sign display.

No hard rules can be given regarding how the advertising dollar should be apportioned in a media mix program. An advertiser spending $5000 or more per month should certainly devote 10% of that total budget to his on-premise signage advertising program in conjunction with his other media efforts. An advertiser spending anywhere from $2000 to $5000 a month should devote 25% to 30% of his budget to the on-premise signage part of his advertising. Very small advertisers might well spend 50% or more on the on-premise sign advertising, since they cannot compete for space and time in other local media but, via their on-premise signs, they can effectively compete with larger retailers; a small business might even have a better location on a higher traffic street and therefore have an advantage over its competitors.

The low cost and high quality of plastics mean that durable signs can be made at a price that even a small merchant can afford. In our period of economic inflation, small retailers have an extremely difficult time starting and staying in business. Table 6 presents the failure rates of small businesses. Signs offer these businesses marked advantages over other advertising media.

Most small merchants have a small, fixed trade area. Their immediate need is for a communication medium that reaches the population of their trade area. If a small business chooses radio advertising or a newspaper display advertisement, wide coverage is obtained. The merchant who chooses these relatively costly media may be paying for unnecessary coverage because he is paying to communicate with people who may never be customers because they live outside the trade area of his business. These people have opportunities to shop at similar places which are much more convenient to them. It is unreasonable to expect these people to go out of their way for goods or services which are already available in their own vicinity.

TABLE 6
Failure Distribution by Liability Size

	Liabilities under $5,000		Liabilities $5,000 to $25,000		Liabilities $25,000 to $100,000		Liabilities $100,000 to $1 Million		Liabilities over $1 Million	
	Number	%	Number	%	Number	%	Number	%	Number	%
1945	270	33.4%	343	42.4%	146	18.0%	45	5.6%	5	0.6%
1946	263	23.3%	488	43.2%	252	22.3%	119	10.6%	7	0.6%
1947	600	17.3%	1,661	47.8%	842	24.2%	350	10.1%	21	0.6%
1948	846	16.1%	2,799	53.3%	1,208	23.0%	374	7.1%	23	0.5%
1949	1,915	20.7%	4,646	50.3%	2,147	23.2%	520	5.6%	18	0.2%
1950	2,065	22.5%	4,706	51.4%	1,975	21.6%	407	4.4%	9	0.1%
1951	1,832	22.7%	4,160	51.6%	1,634	20.3%	412	5.1%	20	0.3%
1952	1,428	18.8%	3,884	51.0%	1,769	23.3%	512	6.7%	18	0.2%
1953	1,383	15.6%	4,317	48.7%	2,375	26.8%	748	8.5%	39	0.4%
1954	1,640	14.8%	5,640	50.9%	2,946	26.5%	829	7.5%	31	0.3%
1955	1,785	16.3%	5,412	49.3%	2,916	26.6%	820	7.5%	36	0.3%
1956	2,032	16.0%	6,152	48.4%	3,431	27.1%	1,022	8.1%	49	0.4%
1957	2,001	14.6%	6,699	48.8%	3,847	28.0%	1,147	8.3%	45	0.3%
1958	2,028	13.5%	7,015	46.9%	4,456	29.8%	1,408	9.4%	57	0.4%
1959	1,841	13.1%	6,664	47.4%	4,202	29.9%	1,284	9.1%	62	0.5%
1960	1,688	10.9%	6,884	44.6%	5,078	32.9%	1,703	11.0%	92	0.6%
1961	1,903	11.1%	7,378	43.2%	5,725	33.5%	1,973	11.6%	96	0.6%
1962	1,647	10.4%	6,700	42.5%	5,425	34.4%	1,876	11.9%	134	0.8%
1963	1,296	9.0%	5,781	40.2%	5,115	35.6%	2,031	14.1%	151	1.1%
1964	1,093	8.1%	5,202	38.5%	5,051	37.4%	2,003	14.9%	152	1.1%
1965	1,007	7.5%	5,067	37.5%	5,266	39.0%	2,005	14.8%	169	1.2%
1966	932	7.1%	4,569	35.0%	5,332	40.8%	2,042	15.7%	186	1.4%
1967	814	6.6%	4,434	35.9%	4,896	39.6%	2,045	16.5%	175	1.4%
1968	481	5.0%	3,332	34.6%	4,016	41.7%	1,686	17.5%	121	1.2%
1969	416	4.6%	3,000	32.8%	3,776	41.2%	1,807	19.7%	155	1.7%
1970	430	4.0%	3,197	29.7%	4,392	40.9%	2,450	22.8%	279	2.6%
1971	392	3.8%	2,806	27.2%	4,413	42.7%	2,423	23.5%	292	2.8%
1972	394	4.1%	2,497	26.1%	4,149	43.4%	2,236	23.4%	290	3.0%
1973	285	3.0%	2,434	26.1%	3,908	41.8%	2,375	25.4%	343	3.7%
1974	304	3.1%	2,150	21.7%	4,279	43.1%	2,755	27.8%	427	4.3%
1975	292	2.5%	2,226	19.5%	4,986	43.6%	3,459	30.3%	469	4.1%
1976	122	1.3%	1,750	18.2%	4,304	44.7%	3,029	31.4%	423	4.4%
1977	102	1.3%	1,283	16.2%	3,476	43.9%	2,708	34.2%	350	4.4%
1978	76	1.2%	928	14.0%	2,708	40.9%	2,593	39.2%	314	4.7%
1979	62	0.8%	954	12.6%	2,914	38.5%	3,216	42.5%	418	5.6%
1980	72	0.6%	1,243	10.6%	4,367	37.2%	5,417	46.1%	643	5.5%
1981	118	0.7%	1,862	11.1%	6,253	37.2%	7,648	45.6%	913	5.4%
1982	141	0.6%	2,789	11.2%	8,579	34.4%	11,737	47.1%	1,662	6.7%
1983	1,065	3.4%	4,167	13.3%	10,340	33.0%	13,851	44.2%	1,911	6.1%
1984	16,095	30.9%	5,489	10.5%	11,943	22.9%	15,723	30.2%	2,828	5.4%
1985	19,028	33.2%	5,287	9.2%	12,236	21.4%	17,359	30.3%	3,343	5.8%
1986p	21,790	35.6%	4,548	7.4%	12,487	20.4%	18,749	30.6%	3,658	6.0%

Due to statistical revision, data prior to 1984 are not directly comparable with the new series.
p = preliminary

Source: The Dun & Bradstreet Corp.

Chapter Nine:

STANDARD MEASURES OF MEDIA EFFECTIVENESS

Large national advertisers use standard measures to evaluate the effectiveness of media in communicating a message to the market. These standard measures are also applicable to signs. This makes comparison among media possible for the local business person who wishes to plan how best to allocate a limited advertising budget.

Reach

Reach is the term applied to the total number of people who are exposed to an advertising message. It is important for the business person to know how many people a particular medium can reach. This figure is also important in determining the potential trade area.

In order to calculate the number of potential viewers of a sign, it is necessary to obtain both vehicular and pedestrian traffic counts. These counts are adjusted by appropriate mathematical formulas to yield accurate estimates. Reach also refers to the trade area serviced by the sign. It is possible to draw a dot map which will describe the trade area serviced by a sign.

Coverage

The coverage of a market by a particular advertising medium refers to the percentage of the total market population represented by all the different people who are reached by a message displayed in a given medium. Often, businesses are interested in learning what percentage of a market is not reached by a message so they can decide how to reach this group if the market potential seems significant.

Because of basic differences in advertising media, the techniques used for assessing coverage in different media show significant differences. For example, to find out the market coverage for a local newspaper, the daily circulation of the paper can be compared to the number of households in the total market. **Standard Rate and Data** is a reference book which contains statistics for many newspapers. Advertising agencies use this book to compare the rates and coverage of various newspapers.

The coverage of a local market for any form of outdoor advertising is, by comparison to newspaper coverage, more complicated to discover. Basically, there are two methods: 1) conduct a survey; and 2) analyze traffic information. The survey involves contacting local residents and inquiring into their habits and patterns of travel when going to work, doing errands, shopping, etc. Traffic information is normally made available by the city or state. Many cities make available maps that show the daily traffic count on local highways and streets.

Information from a survey could be combined with traffic data to draw useful conclusions. If, for example, a map indicated that 20,000 vehicles used Main Street each day (600,000 per month), and if from surveys it is known that the average frequency of trips was 20 per month, it is then possible to determine that each month 30,000 different vehicles use Main Street.

In a town with a population of 25,000, an on-premise sign on Main Street will have very high coverage. About 85% of the people in that trade area (from the city and the surrounding area) will make at least one trip past that sign in a month.

A local newspaper in a town that size will go to about 50% or 60% of the homes in the market. This means that as many as 40% to 50% of the market will never see a message printed in the newspaper. The number of people reached by a radio advertisement is even less. If a local retailer uses one commercial per day, the market coverage for the message would be determined by estimating how many people were tuned in to the station at the minute when the message was broadcast. This portion might be between 1% and 5% of the total market.

FIGURE 6
Tracking Media Dollars

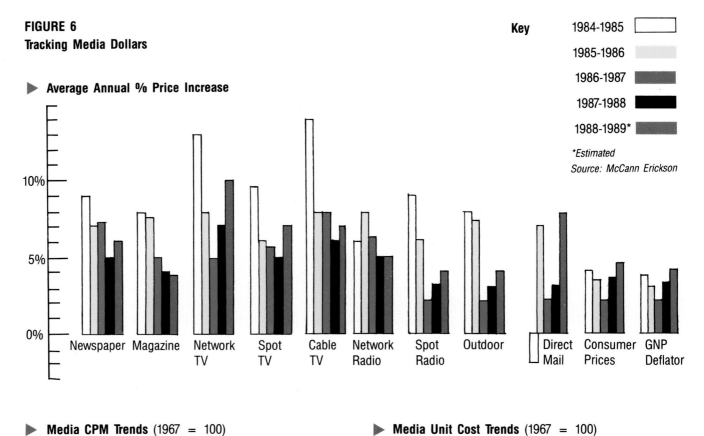

▶ **Average Annual % Price Increase**

Key
1984-1985
1985-1986
1986-1987
1987-1988
1988-1989*

*Estimated
Source: McCann Erickson

Newspaper Magazine Network TV Spot TV Cable TV Network Radio Spot Radio Outdoor Direct Mail Consumer Prices GNP Deflator

▶ **Media CPM Trends** (1967 = 100)

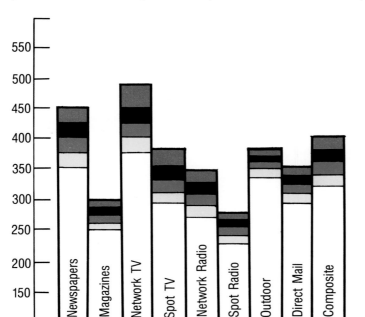

Newspapers · Magazines · Network TV · Spot TV · Network Radio · Spot Radio · Outdoor · Direct Mail · Composite

▶ **Media Unit Cost Trends** (1967 = 100)

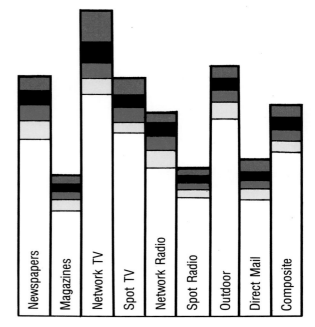

Newspapers · Magazines · Network TV · Spot TV · Network Radio · Spot Radio · Outdoor · Direct Mail · Composite

Note: Units in the media listed include: a single B&W page for newspapers; a four-color ad for magazines; 30-second spots for network and spot TV; 60-second spots for network and spot radio;

a 100 showing in outdoor (100 gross ratings points, which is the reach and frequency of X amount of boards per day); 25,000 pieces of direct mail.

Source: McCann Erickson copyright 1987 by Crain Communications, Inc. reprinted in the Nov. 30, 1987 issue of Advertising Age, page S4.

Frequency

Frequency refers to how often the same person receives an advertising message in a specified time interval. It is the classic measure of repetition. In order to guarantee a large number of market exposures for an advertising message, an advertiser often has to repeat his message. If, for example, in a month he wanted the market to have 10 exposures to a newspaper message, then advertising would have to be scheduled for 10 different days in that month.

To determine the frequency of exposures from signs, it is important to know something about the location of the advertising and the travel patterns of the people in the market. If a segment of the market goes to work along a certain road each day, and if this route takes them past the sign, then the number of days that people go to work is the frequency of repeated exposures to the advertising. A great many studies have been made of travel patterns and habits in business districts. In these studies, reliable averages have been consistently found. A typical on-premise sign in a business district will be passed a minimum of 12 times in one month by the average market-area resident. It is important to note here that the travel patterns of Americans have become extremely concentrated.

Realtors recognize the importance that traffic circulation has for a business location. Often, in commercial areas, the price of the property is calculated in terms of the frontage-foot, because it is so important for businesses to have as large a number of people passing by them as possible.

Cost-Per-Thousand Exposures

Cost-per-thousand exposures refers to how much it costs an advertiser to send a message to 1000 receivers. This measure is calculated by dividing the amount of money spent for a given advertisement by the number of people known to have been exposed to it. Signs excel any other advertising medium in delivering low cost-per-thousand exposures because they are a relatively permanent part of the landscape. Unlike newspapers and magazines, which circulate to their customers, signs have a fixed point, and the audience moves around them. Unlike radio and television, signs include a very great number of repeated "announcements" for one initial investment. Figure 6 provides a comparison of typical monthly advertising costs across six media.

When comparing the cost-per-thousand exposures for different media, it should be remembered that for each medium, the cost is calculated in a distinct manner. In other words, the number of newspapers sold is used in calculating the number of exposures for a newspaper; when television exposures are calculated, the number of sets turned on is projected. For signs, the number of exposures is based on the number of vehicles traveling past the sign.

Recognition

Recognition refers to the ability of an advertisement to be known or identified by a viewer. The degree of recognition of an advertisement is related to the frequency of exposure. This particular assessment of commercial communication sometimes proves to be a major problem for businesses that offer a standard line of products or standardized services. Many companies have developed logos to promote instant recognition. However, these logo identification programs must face the problem of habituation. This term refers to the way we fail to "see" things in our everyday surroundings once they have become familiar to us.

Many companies must resort to various combinations of advertising media in an effort to maintain the public's awareness of their company symbols. On-premise signs counter habituation in three ways. First, signs identify something that a person might not otherwise notice, such as a small hardware store. It is in this context that an illuminated on-premise sign is so important and necessary. There is a marked difference between its day and nighttime appearance. In fact, in a California court hearing, one of the state's major furniture manufacturers said he could survive financially without any other form of advertising if he were only allowed to keep his large on-premise sign lit at night.

Another step to avoid habituation is to use a sign which changes in some way, such as one which changes its color. Different displays are introduced as the colors change from day- to night-viewing conditions.

Finally, when the advertiser has a way of selecting and changing copy, habituation can be averted. Psychologists would describe this as a change in stimulus. In a sense, the eyes perceive a new sign. This becomes possible when letters can be changed manually or electronically.

With its repetition of exposures and message changes, a marquee draws attention. This is one reason that sign artists select a primary message and only then find effective ways to get that message reinforced. When Ford Motor Company runs a television advertisement, the message concludes with a brief look at the company's sign. The intention is that when television viewers see such a sign, they will recognize it and remember what they have just seen and heard.

Impact

Another requirement of advertising in any media (but only recently in signs) is impact. This refers to the achievement of advertising goals. Sometimes signs display the same message used in other media to enhance impact.

Readership

Readership has been studied for many years. In fact, newspaper advertising readership has been studied for about the last 50 years. It is known that on the average, a quarter-page advertisement will be read by about 20% of the paper's readers. This means that if the newspaper's circulation covers 50% of the market, the quarter-page ad will be actually read by about 10% (20% x 50%) of the total market.

In a study of the readership of an on-premise sign, customers at a restaurant were interviewed and asked whether they had noticed the sign and the changeable copy message displayed in front of the restaurant. Of the people interviewed, 78% said that they remembered seeing the message on the sign. This does not mean that the 78% figure for readers of the sign can be compared to the 20% who see a quarter-page newspaper advertisement. This particular study is mentioned because no systematic study has compared the readers of an on-premise sign to the total number of people who are exposed to it.

To make a fair comparison between this sign study and a newspaper ad, one would have to go to a business establishment that had run a newspaper ad and find out how many of the customers who were present had read the printed advertisement. In the case of the restaurant sign, eight out of 10 customers said that they had read the sign. Even more important, 20% of the customers said that they had stopped at the restaurant because of the message they had seen on the sign.

In one study by 3M Co., the effectiveness of a changeable copy sign at a Ramada Inn restaurant was compared to a local newspaper ad through a survey. Ten times more respondents remembered seeing the changeable copy sign than recalled seeing the newspaper ad. In this study, the changeable copy display was changed each day to show that day's lunch special and its price. Sales of the higher profit item advertised on the changeable copy sign increased by 83.1% over when it was only listed on the menu. Of those responding, 13.1% said that they were influenced to eat at the Ramada Inn as a result of seeing the readerboard advertising.

Top-of-the-Mind Awareness

The goal of using the information derived from the measures of reach, frequency, cost-per-thousand exposures and other indices is to achieve what has been called top-of-the-mind awareness. This phrase describes the association in a customer's mind between a particular place of business or a brand name and a particular product. Top-of-the-mind awareness is present when a customer names the first store or brand that comes to mind when a given product is mentioned.

Top-of-the-mind awareness is a function of memory and as such is a learning phenomenon. In effect, the consumer learns to associate a particular message with

Warning: The Surgeon General Has Determined That Cigarette Smoking Is Dangerous to Your Health.

CAMEL LIGHTS

LOW TAR
CAMEL TASTE

a given product and a particular product with a given retailer or a given brand name. Advertisers consider the proportion of persons that instantly associates a product with a particular brand name to be a measure of the share of the market which that brand holds. While top-of-the-mind awareness is certainly a useful concept in advertising, there are some qualifications.

Top-of-the-mind awareness has proven to be most applicable to consumer goods that are bought on impulse. It also operates most often when the goods are relatively un-differentiated — i.e., when there is not a great deal of difference between one product and another product in the same category. While many companies certainly base their advertising strategies on this principle, and it is effective in many situations, it cannot be applied across the board.

A retailer who understands the importance of increasing top-of-the-mind awareness may find this increase difficult to achieve. In some markets, scale itself is a problem; it is difficult to "educate" great numbers of people about the advantages of a particular product or place of business. Typically, the population of the market is not fixed in number or in makeup. Both these measures can change rapidly over time. Estimates of the percentage of the average portion of the market population that will be new to an area range from 7% to 20%. Approximately 40 million Americans move each year, which indicates that even well known merchants are obliged to continually keep their names prominent just to keep from losing ground in terms of the public's aware-ness of them. Even in areas where there is little change in population, the advertiser has to combat the tendency of consumers to forget names that may already be familiar.

Impulse Buying Potential

The considerations discussed earlier are those most commonly used to evaluate and compare advertising media, but there are other factors by which advertisers evaluate their decisions about which medium best suits their needs. One way of evaluating a message is to think of the time of day that a message will be seen in relation to the time of day at which the viewer, reader or listener most likely makes a trip to the store. A related means of evaluation is to consider how close the prospective consumer is to the store when he is exposed to the message. These factors are important because of the phenomenon of impulse buying — making purchasing decisions on a sudden impulse rather than with planning and forethought. Surveys consistently show that approximately 40% of the purchases made in supermarkets are the result of impulse decisions. This phenomenon occurs in many other types of markets as well. Because of its importance, the ability of a medium to encourage impulse buying should be con-sidered.

Signs encourage impulse buying by reminding consumers of a product and their need or desire for it right at the place the product may be purchased.

Synergism

Another phenomenon to consider is synergism — the whole equals more than the sum of its parts. It is possible for a combination of several media to produce results that, because of mutual reinforcement, are more than would be expected from adding up the effects of advertising in each of the several media. In the case of signage, this means that an effective on-premise sign may increase consumers' awareness of a par-ticular business and its location, so that if they should see, say, a direct mail advertise-ment, they will be more inclined to read it. Ultimately, this means that the cost of each read/remembered exposure to the direct mail leaflet will be reduced.

GROUPS BENEFITING FROM SIGN ADVERTISING

The important economic functions of on-premise signs may be analyzed according to the groups of people they help. These include: 1) local retailers; 2) convenience stores; 3) national advertisers; 4) consumers; and 5) the community as an economic distribution center in competition with other communities.

Independent businesses dominate the retail world. Photo courtesy of Don Bell & Co., Daytona Beach, FL.

Local Retailers

Independent business dominates the retailing world. According to figures from the US Small Business Administration, approximately 99% of retail trade in the United States is carried out by small business. This means that changes in the retail sector of the economy mean changes in small business. Table 7 summarizes the importance of small

TABLE 7

Share of market as measured by business receipts — 1984

INDUSTRY	NUMBER OF RETURNS	BUSINESS RECEIPTS (x $1,000)
Agriculture services, Forestry, Fishery (Nonfarm)		
Sole Proprietorships	322,924	10,700,001
Partnerships	139,306	5,885,672
Corporations	98,361	62,093,338
Mining		
Sole Proprietorships	153,445	13,190,105
Partnerships	56,548	18,637,767
Corporations	40,564	111,030,063
Construction		
Sole Proprietorships	1,386,099	63,311,253
Partnerships	64,607	23,198,439
Corporations	306,906	326,752,784
Manufacturing		
Sole Proprietorships	320,106	18,176,274
Partnerships	29,606	18,326,382
Corporations	272,050	2,608,971,901
Transportation, Communication, Electric, Gas, and Sanitary Services		
Sole Proprietorships	572,325	29,087,904
Partnerships	20,578	142,091
Corporations	128,184	693,105,168
Wholesale and Retail Trade		
Sole Proprietorships	2,380,838	195,961,164
Partnerships	184,841	72,335,387
Corporations	896,524	2,250,774,641
Finance, Insurance, and Real Estate		
Sole Proprietorships	984,029	29,977,330
Partnerships	790,902	94,362,434
Corporations	497,366	431,157,290
Services		
Sole Proprietorships	4,989,999	147,438,458
Partnerships	331,103	90,243,640
Corporations	899,370	458,038,533
Total Nonfarm Industries		
Sole Proprietorships	11,262,390	516,036,944
Partnerships	1,900,745	357,802,613
Corporations	3,139,325	6,941,923,718

Source: This table was compiled from Statistics of Income, SOI Bulletin, Summer 1986 and Summer 1987, published by the Department of the Treasury, Internal Revenue Service.

This table indicates the importance of small business, including sole proprietorships and partnerships, to the economy of the US by comparing them with corporations. Small businesses far outnumber corporations, although their total business receipts are less. The business receipts of small businesses outnumber the corporation business receipts in the area of wholesale and retail trade.

businesses to the American economy by indicating share of the market. Figure 7 indicates the overall growth of retail sales over 1986-1987.

The sign is the ideal communication medium to integrate national and local systems of advertising. Once a product has been seen in national media advertising, its introduction is complete. The next step in the distribution process is making the availability of the product known. A consumer who knows of and wants a product will also want to know where he can purchase it. The first place he sees featuring the item is likely to be the place where he makes his purchase. On-premise signs show the consumer where to satisfy such newly discovered needs or wants. They are the medium which brings people into a store to buy a product that has already been "sold" to them via national advertising.

Table 8 compares local and national advertising expenditures from 1950 to 1985.

FIGURE 7
Retail Sales
Year-to-Year Percent Change

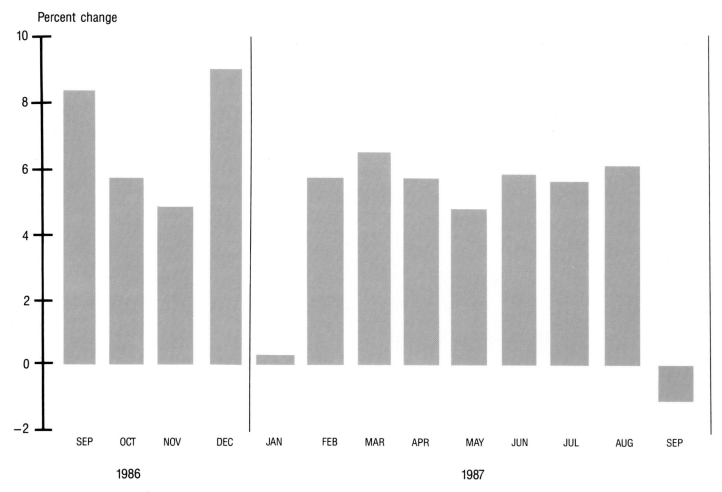

TABLE 8

No. 924. Advertising — Estimated Expenditures: 1950 to 1985

(In millions of dollars. See also Historical Statistics, Colonial Times to 1970, series T 444—446)

YEAR	Total	National	Local	YEAR	Total	National	Local	YEAR	Total	National	Local
1950	5,700	3,260	2,440	1973	24,980	13,700	11,260	1980	53,550	29,815	23,735
1955	9,150	5,380	3,770	1974	26,620	14,700	11,920	1981	60,430	33,890	26,540
1960	11,960	7,305	4,655	1975	27,900	15,200	12,700	1982	66,580	37,765	26,795
1965	15,250	9,340	5,910	1976	33,300	18,355	14,945	1983	75,850	42,525	33,325
1970	19,550	11,350	5,200	1977	37,440	20,595	16,645	1984	87,820	49,690	36,130
1971	20,700	11,755	8,945	1978	43,330	23,720	19,610	1985	94,750	53,355	41,395
1972	23,210	12,960	10,230	1979	48,780	26,695	22,065				

Source: McCann-Erickson, Inc., New York, NY. Compiled for Crain Communications, Inc. in Advertising Age (copyright).
Source: Statistical Abstract of the United States: 1987 Washington, D.C., U.S. Dept. of Commerce, Bureau of the Census, 1986, p. 537.

National Advertisers

Some national advertisers sell their products or services through local retail stores on a non-exclusive basis. Others make sales only through franchise or company-owned retail outlets.

National advertisers can be extremely powerful even when their distribution is non-exclusive if they spend enough on their advertising. They anticipate that their national advertising expenditure will help local retailers. In return, they expect promotional help. Product manufacturers may have tremendous influence with retailers. Retailers can benefit from large national promotions by product manufacturers. If a product that a business sells is being promoted on television, the local retailer can jump on the bandwagon. An on-premise sign can let people know that a business offers all the benefits of the product they have heard so much about and may be predisposed to buy.

Even though the smaller manufacturer can compete in quality and sometimes offers a lower price, it cannot compete in terms of advertising expenditure. Advertising done by leaders in the industry, however, often helps everyone in the industry by promoting the product itself besides the particular brand. A retailer who wants to help promote the products of small manufacturers may also use an on-premise sign.

Franchises

National manufacturers often choose to distribute their goods and services through franchises. Franchise arrangements can be successful in a wide variety of endeavors. At one time, almost all automobile tune-ups were done at gasoline service stations. But in recent years, service stations have been abandoning that service, and this market has attracted franchisers. Insta-Tune, Inc., of California probably led the way in this trend in the early 1970s. The president of Insta-Tune claimed at that time that a typical shop should net $37,100 on sales of $140,000 annually after three years. The total cost of beginning an operation was about $50,000. Franchisees usually receive help in designing and arranging their units. They also frequently receive a training program as well as other forms of assistance such as legal advice and advertising.

For the franchisee in a new business, the on-premise sign is an important advertising asset. It introduces him to the public as a member of a business group whose name may already be familiar because of other advertising, including on-premise signage at other locations. As the chain grows, the value of this asset increases. Through a franchise, an individual operator receives support but still has to attract customers to his particular shop.

National franchises often choose to distribute their goods and services through franchises.

Fast-Food Industry

A special example of an industry that is growing with the franchise arrangement is the fast-food industry. In 1978, of the $50 billion spent on meals away from home, 28% went to the fast-food industry. In 1976, the rate of growth for fast-food sales was 15%. (Maxwell Assoc.; based on Commerce Department data.) Although the food services industry continues to grow, it faces significant problems. Statistics indicate that demographics and industry saturation may be taking a toll on the fast-food restaurant phenomenon. Although 36% of the US adult population ate out on any given day in 1986, this was down from the 37% recorded in 1983-85. Survival in the restaurant business is not easy. Fifty percent of all new restaurants close within one year, and half of the remainder fail in the second year. (Reported by Alex Brown & Sons, Standard & Poor's Industry Surveys, March 26, 1987, p. L37.) Fast-food franchises may have an edge over other food services that do not have the advantage of national corporate advertising.

Aided by the franchising phenomenon, more than 60 fast-food or chain restaurants had at least 200 units each in 1986, according to *Entrepreneur* magazine, including 15 with more than 1000 each. Of the 62 chains with a combined total of 78,000 outlets, 73% were operated by franchisees.

The fast-food industry has become almost a cultural phenomenon in the US — with literally thousands of outlets and no end in sight.

McDonald's has long been at the top of the list of fast-food chains. (Table 9 shows the top 25 food service chains.) In 1985 McDonald's accounted for approximately 20% of the total sales in the fast-food industry with a $3.1 billion worldwide sales base and about 4200 outlets. (Maxwell Assoc.; based on Commerce Department data.) In 1986, McDonald's US systemwide sales of close to $10 billion accounted again for about 20% of fast-food sales. At the end of 1986 there were 2272 franchised and company-owned McDonald's restaurants in the US and 2138 in foreign countries. (Standard & Poor's Industry Surveys, March 26, 1987, p. L36.)

Initially, McDonald's located outlets only within a three-mile radius of an area with a population of 50,000. In the early 1970s, research showed that the majority of customers stopped on their way to some activity or on a trip. Acting on this information, McDonald's changed its strategy and began locating sites according to patterns of potential customer activity. McDonald's lead in the fast-food industry has been greatly attributed to its marketing clout. (Standard & Poor's Industry Surveys, March 26, 1987, p. L36.) The golden arches sign of McDonald's is an indispensable and recognizable aspect of the company's national advertising campaign. A business must be careful, however, before allotting a large percentage of its budget to advertising. Until a business is of sufficient size to justify the expense, a large advertising budget may be a mis-

TABLE 9

Top 25 food-service chains — 1985
(Ranked by systemwide food-service sales)

[5]Rank	Chain	Chain headquarters	[6]Concept	Parent company	Fiscal year ends	[7]Systemwide sales (By fiscal year, in millions of $)		Number of units
						[8]Last full	[9]Previous	
1.	McDonald's	Oak Brook, Ill.	Burger	McDonald's Corp.	Dec.	11,000.0	10,000.0	9,460
2.	Burger King	Miami, Fla.	Burger	Pillsbury Co.	May	4,500.0	3,990.0	5,108
3.	Kentucky Fried Chicken	Louisville, Ky.	Chicken	PepsiCo Inc.	Dec.	3,100.0	2,800.0	6,729
4.	Wendy's	Dublin, Ohio	Burger	Wendy's International	Dec.	2,690.0	2,420.0	3,842
5.	Hardee's	Rocky Mount, N.C.	Burger	Imasco Ltd.	March	2,400.0	2,220.0	2,835
6.	Pizza Hut	Wichita, Kan.	Pizza	PepsiCo Inc.	Dec.	1,880.0	1,600.0	5,200
7.	Marriott Food Service[1]	Bethesda, Md.	Contract	Marriott Corp.	Dec.	1,586.3	1,069.5	2,580
8.	Dairy Queen	Minneapolis, Minn.	Ice Cream	Int'l. Dairy Queen Inc.	Nov.	1,546.0	1,391.0	4,900
9.	ARA Services	Philadelphia, Pa.	Contract	ARA Services Inc.	Sept.	1,299.3	1,241.0	2,020
10.	Taco Bell	Irvine, Calif.	Taco	PepsiCo Inc.	Dec.	1,155.2	954.5	2,423
11.	Sheraton	Boston, Mass.	Hotel	ITT Corp.	Dec.	1,162.9	1,095.0	507
12.	Domino's	Ann Arbor, Mich.	Pizza	Domino's Pizza Inc.	Dec.	1,084.0	626.0	3,950
13.	Big Boy	Glendale, Calif.	Fam. Rest.	Marriott Corp.	Dec.	1,061.3	1,100.0	958
14.	Denny's	La Mirada, Calif.	Fam. Rest.	DHI Corp.	June	1,000.0	1,060.0	1,175
15.	Holiday Inn	Memphis, Tenn.	Hotel	Holiday Corp.	Dec.	907.6	893.1	1,692
16.	Hilton	Beverly Hills, Calif.	Hotel	Hilton Hotels Corp.	Dec.	893.0	812.3	291
17.	Red Lobster	Orlando, Fla.	Dinnerhouse	General Mills Inc.	May	875.0	827.0	400
18.	Arby's	Atlanta, Ga.	Roast Beef	Royal Crown Cos.	Dec.	814.0	760.0	1,710
19.	Marriott Hotel	Bethesda, Md.	Hotel	Marriott Corp.	Dec.	716.0	697.0	165
20.	Long John Silver's	Lexington, Ky.	Fish	Jerrico Inc.	June	693.0	637.3	1,459
21.	Ponderosa[3]	Dayton, Ohio	Fam. Steak.	Ponderosa Inc.	Feb.	677.1	694.7	697
22.	Church's	San Antonio, Tex.	Chicken	Church's Fried Chicken	Dec.	639.9	633.8	1,585
23.	Shoney's	Nashville, Tenn.	Fam. Rest.	Shoney's Inc.	Oct.	590.0	514.3	581
24.	Canteen[2]	Chicago, Ill.	Contract	Transworld Corp.	Dec.	578.6	429.1	1,900
25.	Dunkin' Donuts	Braintree, Mass.	Doughnut	Dunkin' Donuts Inc.	Oct.	576.7	532.1	1,557

[1]Marriott Food Service Management includes a prorated share of Saga Corp.'s fiscal year results. [2]Canteen estimates reflect acquisition of Interstate United in October 1985. [3]Dobbs estimates include results from Dobbs Houses, Dobbs International Services, Carson International and Ridgewell's Inc. [4]Service America estimates include results from Macke and Servomation. [5]Rank is based on Last Full Fiscal Year systemwide sales. [6]Chains are classified based on their popular perception, best-selling entree or market positioning. [7]Net sales at all units operating under the chain name. Includes both company-owned and franchised units. Excludes franchise fees, interest income, manufacturing and distribution sales and other revenue not directly resulting from food and beverage sales. [8]Last Full Fiscal Year is the fiscal year most recently completed prior to Aug. 11, 1986. Most often it is calendar year 1985. [9]Previous Fiscal Year is the year before the Last Full Fiscal Year. Most often, calendar 1984.

Source: Nation's Restaurant News.

take. Wendy's, the fourth largest food service chain in 1985, did not begin major media advertising until April of 1977 when the company had 660 outlets in 150 major markets. Wendy's has climbed to fourth from 18th in 1977. On-premise signage helps to meet the needs of advertisers who are not yet able to spend millions of dollars on network media advertising.

Consumers

Our economic system is characterized by many individual decisions concerning individual purchases. In order to make satisfactory choices, consumers need information. The growth of consumerism as a recognized movement has increased the pressure on manufacturers and distributors to make information available. Given the patterns of distribution in our economy, advertising is the local means of disseminating information of this type. A 1976 Supreme Court decision upheld the notion of advertising as a protected civil right because it is a means of disseminating information (*Virginia State Board of Pharmacy v. Virginia Citizens' Consumer Council*, 425 U.S. 748 (1976)). The words of the decision emphasize the importance of the free flow of information in our society: "Advertising, however tasteless and excessive it sometimes may seem, is nonetheless dissemination of information as to who is producing and selling what product, for what reason, and at what price. So long as we preserve a predominantly free enterprise economy, the allocation of our resources in large measure will be made through numerous, private economic decisions. It is a matter of public interest that those decisions, in the aggregate, be intelligent and well informed. To this end, the free flow of economic information is indispensable."

Sometimes business people discover too late that they have failed to provide consumers with very basic information that they want and need. Marshall Field & Company of Chicago, for example, operated for 70 years without ever installing a floor plan. Customers were somehow expected to know their way around the store's 2.2 million sq. ft. Between 1972 and 1976 its earnings fell 10%. Marshall Field & Company realized its error and made efforts to make its stores more customer-friendly. The efforts were successful. In 1987, with 25 locations in Wisconsin, Illinois and Texas, the company surpassed the $1 billion mark for sales. (Marshall Field & Company, Special Events Department Statistics.)

Communities

On-premise signs contribute to the economic viability of a community by helping business, especially small business, meet the information needs of its customers. Communities are becoming aware of this function of signs and recognizing that in many cases their business community can be helped by a sign code that allows local merchants the signage they need. Since communities, in effect, compete for shoppers, signs can give a particular town or city a competitive advantage over its neighbors.

Several benefits result from the economic vitality of a local business district. The psychological advantage of having a prosperous town is usually obvious. But in many places, there are also practical reasons for encouraging retail trade. In the state of California, for example, individual cities receive a rebate from the state sales tax paid in their community. Signs are extremely attractive to communities in this capacity; they can generate revenues and require almost no municipal services in return.

Signs Set a Mood or Express a Theme

At the opposite extreme from professional office areas are zones characterized by concentrated commercial, predominantly nighttime, activity. Las Vegas can be seen as the prototype of such zones. The needs of these zones can also be satisfied by signs in a different way. This difference attests to the fact that a sign program has a multi-faceted function. In nearly every metropolitan area, there is a zone characterized by diversity and a great deal of activity. For these zones, signs help set the mood. In these areas, they do not provide information that has direct impact, but their cumulative effect is significant.

In the function of setting tone, signs also help encourage movement between one establishment and another. This function became particularly apparent during the last energy crisis in Las Vegas. At that time, in an act of unprecedented cooperation, casino owners in Las Vegas agreed to use only the reader board portion of their signs. Their attitude was strictly practical. Casino owners reasoned that patrons would drive around town reading the various signs, especially reader boards and outdoor advertising displays, to find out what shows were playing and then select a casino based on that information. They thought that turning off the major portion of the signs would have minimal effects.

The results, however, were rather startling. The signs were found to function as a directional system. Without the brightly lit festive atmosphere, the customer activity was severely curtailed. The signs facilitated the movement of people among the casinos at night. The fact that the area was brightly lit with commercial communication about particular activities provided encouragement for those very activities. The sign was a symbol of the festive atmosphere and at the same time actually contributed to it.

ASSESSING THE SIGNAGE NEEDS OF A BUSINESS

Market Research

Before an effective sign can be designed, a person must know the signage needs of his business. For instance, if potential customers are expected to come largely from out-of-town and are unfamiliar with the area, a sign which can aid in directing them to the business will be needed. Perhaps potential customers are drawn to a store because of its discount prices. In that case, the sign must advertise that the store has low prices. Before any decisions can be made on what kind of signs to use, how large they will be, what copy will be displayed and what overall graphic design to use, marketing information will be needed.

FIGURE 8
Trade Area Map

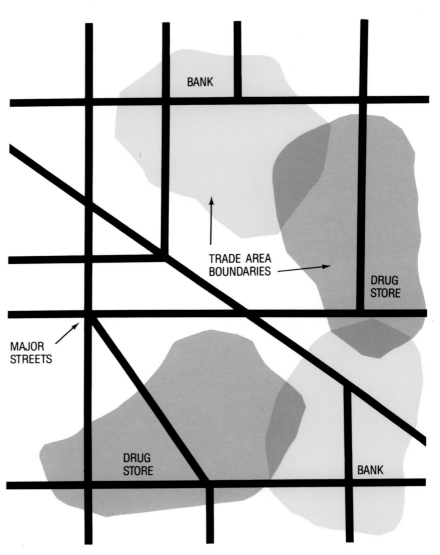

Figure 8 is an illustration of hypothetical trade area boundaries showing typical irregularity of shape and overlap. A simple trade area map can be made for any small business. Most retailing customers are drawn to a business from the surrounding trade area by the on-premise sign.

Defining the Trade Area

Most retailers, small businesses especially, draw their customers from a geographically defined area surrounding the business location. The trade area should be defined so the merchant will know where to direct his advertising in order to attract customers. A signage program can provide a certain percentage of coverage of the trade area.

There are procedures that have been established to evaluate the potential sales volume of a trade area. Some of these procedures are quite complex and will not be discussed here. (For a detailed overview of retail site selection and the evaluation of procedures, the reader is referred to **The Mobile Consumer**, a book based on extensive retailing studies by R.J. Claus [1972].) Most trade associations can provide information on the typical trade area size for a given type of retailing. These estimates can help to plot an approximate trade area for a business.

The trade area map

A simple procedure for establishing the trade area for a small business is outlined below.
1) Obtain a local street map;
2) Mark the location of the site on the map;
3) Drive 15 minutes from the site in all four directions and mark the map.

Figure 8 provides a rough outline to help you determine from where most of your customers will be coming.

Estimating potential volume

Census records and data available from local governments or Chambers of Commerce and credit bureaus will provide the basis for calculating gross potential sales volume in a trade area. Obtain data on the following variables for the area you have marked on the map:
1) Population:
   Number of households
   Number of persons
2) Income:
   Average household
   Average per capita
3) Type of area:
   Residential (apartment or single family)
   Commercial/Industrial
4) Percentage of growth in area
5) Number of competitors in area
6) Sales volume of competitors in area
7) Credit representation in area: (number of bank cards, travel cards, charge accounts, etc.)
8) Number of units in area directly related to business

From this information a merchant can estimate the total volume potential of his business trade area.

Locating Your Customers

After your business has begun, make a practice of noting the home addresses of customers from checks, charges and other records. This has two advantages: it helps define the trade area, and it provides a mailing list for promotions. Customer addresses can be plotted on the trade area map and the shape of the trade area adjusted to correspond with the data.

The trade area tells what kind of sign is needed. When it is known how a trade area is shaped, it is possible to tell from which directions the sign must be visible. The type of sign selected should correspond to site visibility needs.

The trade area map will also tell which nearby streets are sources for customers. The small business owner will want to obtain street profiles.

Determining Traffic Flow

It is important for a business person to know the average number of vehicles that pass his store in a 24-hour period. This figure forms the basis for a number of calculations which determine sign effectiveness. The average 24-hour traffic volume can be obtained from a city, county or state traffic engineering office.

Traffic flow maps are not usually printed on an annual basis, so it is important to ask for a recent estimate of the street or to calculate a recent estimate using a 5% annual growth rate. Also, traffic flow counts are taken at given points which may or may not be close to the particular business. An estimate of the two-way traffic flow from the two nearest points in front of the business is also necessary.

Load Factor

The traffic flow will only tell you how many autos pass your business in a 24-hour period; it will not tell you how many people pass by. A street profile will help determine the traffic load factor. Average load factors for incorporated areas are 1.7 to 1.9 people per car. For unincorporated areas, the average is 2 per car, and during vacation seasons the load factor rises to 3.5 people per car.

It's important for the business person to know the average number of vehicles that pass his store in a 24-hour period. Photo courtesy of Ad Art, Inc., Stockton, CA.

Determining the Street Profile

Most retail business people intuitively appreciate the importance of traffic in relation to business. They think about the volume of traffic that passes a site when they choose their location. They know that every person who passes the store is a potential customer. But, that is usually the extent of their interest in traffic. Rarely does a business person go beyond his awareness of traffic volume to an awareness of the importance of traffic profile. Traffic engineering data, available locally, can also provide useful information in this critically important area.

A street profile not only describes the amount of traffic passing a business, it also gives the type of traffic involved. It provides useful facts about different conditions, such as the time of day or the season of the year, that may affect the traffic flow patterns. Usually this information is in the form of origin-destination studies. Such studies provide information that is likely to indicate:

1) Origin and destination: where people begin and end trips.
2) How people travel: by private automobile, public transit, truck, bicycle, on foot, and what percentages.
3) When travel occurs: by hour of day.
4) Reasons for travel: to work, to shop, to school.
5) Where people are traveling to work.
6) Speed of travel: how fast the vehicles are actually traveling.

These studies are usually undertaken to help plan street systems, such as the number of lanes needed, or in assessing the need for public transportation. Any city, county or state traffic engineer has information of this sort, or the business person can obtain data from the Institute of Traffic Engineers.

Knowing about the volume, and more importantly the nature, of the traffic passing each day makes planning the sign message more effective. If, for example, a great many tourists and vacationers pass by, a characteristically local product could be featured on a changeable copyboard or window. Signs can be used to attract customers to a local specialty.

Studies conducted on a number of types of retail establishments have shown that traffic counts alone will accurately predict a large proportion of the volume of a retail site. (Claus, R.J., and Hardwick, W. **The Mobile Consumer: Automobile-Oriented Retailing and Site Selection**. Don Mills, Ontario: Collier-Macmillan Canada, 1972.) This is particularly important in automobile-oriented retailing.

Most retail people intuitively appreciate the importance of traffic in relation to a business. Photo courtesy of Buttrick White & Burris, Architects & Planners, New York, NY.

SECTION 4

Figure 9 illustrates the major types of regulations faced by sign users and the requisite burdens of pleading, production and persuasion. By analyzing each regulation in terms of its public purpose and burden of proof it is possible to establish a strategy for countering any regulation that works an undue hardship on the community. By reference to these factors it is also possible to develop workable regulations which enhance land-use planning goals and the viability of commerce.

Figure 9 also summarizes the shift of burden of proof from the user to the state — whichever has the burden of producing and authenticating evidence that will convince an adjudicator or a jury that the facts they have presented are the truth.

FIGURE 9
BURDEN OF PROOF CONTINUUM
Requisite Burdens of Pleading, Production and Persuasion
for Major Types of Sign Regulations

Public Purpose:	Police Power Basis for Regulation		Constitutional Limitations on Regulation	
	Protection from Harm	**Promotion of Welfare**	**Necessity for Certain Groups**	**Fundamental Rights**
Reason for regulation:	Threat to public health, safety, morals Nuisance	Preservation of property values Aesthetics: Preservation or protection of something pleasing	Required for welfare of certain groups: Zoning of residential, commercial, industrial uses for viability	Clear and present danger of direct threat to public safety or national security
Burden of proof:	Heavy burden on user to prove not dangerous or not a nuisance	Burden on user to prove not nuisance-like activity No police power purpose or activity benefits outweigh aesthetics/nuisance-like claim	Burden on state to prove rational basis or real and substantial basis for regulation Time, place and manner	Strict scrutiny test: Heavy burden on state to prove compelling state interest or clear and present danger
Pleadings:	No danger or nuisance No valid public purpose	No valid police power purpose More value to continuing use	Suspect classes: Handicapped Old Visually impaired	No state interest in suppressing First Amendment protected speech: Political Commercial No time, place, manner restrictions
Production: Types of evidence needed	Traffic/transportation studies Information processing studies Public service (voting, charity) Urban noise/visual clutter	Traffic/transportation studies Information processing studies Public service (voting, charity) Urban noise/visual clutter Asset value Advertising effectiveness Segments of business benefitted	Public service (voting, charity) Asset value Advertising effectiveness Segments of business benefitted	Public service (voting, charity) Segments of business benefitted
Persuasion:	"By clear, strong and convincing evidence" Possibly "beyond a reasonable doubt"	Preponderance or "by clear, strong and convincing evidence"	Preponderance	Preponderance or no burden of persuasion

In most litigation, it is the plaintiff who is seeking to change the present state of affairs, and who must bear the risk of failure in proof or persuasion. Three burdens are assigned to any litigant: 1) pleading; 2) producing evidence; and 3) persuading the judge or jury. (Cleary **Supra**. at 948.) A litigant who cannot carry all of these burdens is likely to lose his case.

There are three traditional formulas for measuring the burden of persuasion:

1) The evidence for a general run of issues in civil cases, "by a preponderance of the evidence," or "greater weight;" 2)"by a clear, strong and convincing evidence" where there are exceptional controversies in civil cases; and 3) "beyond a reasonable doubt" in criminal prosecutions.

For sign code litigation, the "preponderance" standard will be required. Proof by preponderance is proof that leads a jury to find the existence of a contested fact more probable than its nonexistence. In other words, evidence preponderates when it is more convincing than opposing evidence.

Authority For Sign Regulations

The right of a city to regulate signage derives from the state's police powers and from state enabling acts which give the municipality the right to zone. (Hagman and Juergensmeyer, **Urban Planning and Land Development Control Law**, 2d, § 3.6 (1986).) There must be a valid public purpose for the exercise of police powers.

Protection from harm: The most severe use of the police powers occurs when the purpose is to protect the public from harm. The specific reason for a regulation in this category is that the regulated use is a threat to public health, safety or morals or is a nuisance. Under any of these conditions a municipality can immediately abate the use without paying the owner compensation. This means that if a sign is classed as unsafe or as a nuisance it can be taken down immediately, and the owner has no rights to recover. Indeed, the owner may have to pay for the removal.

1) Burden of proof: The user has a very heavy burden of proof when a sign is classed as a threat to public health, safety or morals or is a nuisance. The user must prove by strong evidence presented in court that the sign is not harmful to the public. A sign should never be allowed to be classed a nuisance. There is no property right in a nuisance.

2) Pleadings: Pleadings should stress that the sign is not a danger or nuisance. Signs contribute to the community.

3) Production of evidence: The burden of production concerns two major types of evidence — direct evidence and circumstantial evidence. Evidence must reach the standard that a reasonable man is able to infer that the facts exist from the evidence presented. Under severe police power regulation to protect the public from harm, it is necessary that the type of evidence presented is extremely clear and of these general types. Certainly traffic and transportation studies that show that signs in general are not dangerous or nuisances should be introduced along with specific studies on the particular signs involved. In addition, information processing studies about how the eye sees and how people perceive information in the environment would be important. Public service information such as voting and charity uses of signs would also be appropriate. Any studies that would refute the concept of urban noise or visual clutter would be indispensable. In addition, it might be helpful to discuss the asset value, advertising effectiveness and the segments of the community that are benefitted by the signage. This might include a discussion of tax bases and revenue derived from businesses that are utilizing signs.

4) Burden of persuasion: Since there may be possible criminal sanctions if the sign is found to truly be a threat to public health or safety, and there may be serious violations involved, the standard for satisfying the burden of persuasion will be very high in these types of cases. Generally, in problematical civil litigation, the standard is "by clear, strong and convincing evidence." If there is a criminal violation involved, the burden of persuasion will have to reach the level of "beyond a reasonable doubt."

Promotion of welfare: Most sign regulation falls under the police power rationale of promoting public welfare or preserving property values. Aesthetic regulation falls under this use of the police powers. Preservation or protection of something pleasing has been upheld as a valid police power purpose. (See *Metromedia*.) Signs regulated under the promotion of welfare rationale can be amortized without compensation. That is, the user will be allowed a specified time of continued use in lieu of compensation.

1) Burden of proof: The burden of proof is on the user to prove that the sign is not a "nuisance-like" activity.

2) Pleadings: Pleadings should stress that there is either no valid police power purpose in the regulation or that the benefits of the sign outweigh the aesthetics or the "nuisance-like" claim — there is more value in the continuing use of the sign than there is in its removal.

3) Production of evidence: The burden of producing evidence for challenges to regulations which are based on promotion of public welfare probably requires the heaviest investment of expert time and testimony. Not only must the challenger produce the types of evidence that are necessary in a threat to public safety type of regulation, but in this case, he must also demonstrate that the sign has value to the business, be able to demonstrate the general advertising effectiveness of a sign, and must be able to document which segments of the community are benefitted by the use of signs. Challengers have not only their greatest obligation as far as the range of evidence that should be presented, but also their greatest opportunity to present evidence showing that signs are beneficial to the community and to possibly change attitudes of regulators concerning the value of signage.

4) Burden of persuasion: The burden of persuasion in this type of civil litigation is usually a preponderance of the evidence, or by clear, strong and convincing evidence.

Constitutional Limitations on Regulation

The United States Constitution provides for safeguards against the use of police powers.

Necessity: When a use is a necessity for an identifiable group within a community, a municipality can regulate the use, but must regulate in such as way as to ensure the continued viability of the group. Residential, commercial and industrial users can often be classed into identifiable groups.

1) Burden of proof: The burden is on the state to prove that the regulation has a rational relationship basis or a real and substantial basis.

2) Pleadings: Rational basis for regulation should be attacked, as well as references made to any suspect classes (the aged, handicapped, or visually impaired who are harmed by the regulation).

3) Production of evidence: Production of evidence in this category is not quite as stringent as under the promotion of welfare category. Because the burden of proof has now shifted to the state, the challenger has a much easier responsibility. He needs only to have evidence; he does not need the level of expert testimony required in the previous two situations. Of particular importance in this category would be testimony from the segments of the business and general community that are benefitted by signage, along with any suspect classes that may be benefitted, such as the handicapped, the elderly, infirmed, visually impaired, children or foreigners. The asset value of the sign to the business and to the community would be important to mention here also, along with advertising effectiveness. All of the other rationales should also be stressed.

4) Burden of persuasion: Under this category, a preponderance of the evidence would be the highest level necessary, because the burden is now shifted to the state to refute any statements made by the sign users.

Fundamental rights: Only when there is a clear and present danger of a direct physical threat to the public safety or to national security can a municipality regulate to curtail any fundamental rights such as those protected in the Bill of Rights and under the Fourteenth Amendment Due Process clause.

1) Burden of proof: The state has a heavy burden of proof. The US Supreme Court applies a strict scrutiny test which forces the state to justify a compelling state interest in the regulation. Sometimes proof of a clear and present danger is necessary.

2) Pleadings: Pleadings should stress abridgement of the First Amendment Right of protected speech. Protected speech on signs has been judged political and commercial.

3) Production of Evidence: The types of evidence mentioned earlier apply, but in this case it may not be necessary to produce any evidence except that the freedom of speech has been curtailed and suppressed. If freedom of speech has been suppressed, it is necessary to show the severe effect on the property (the income rights of a business) or the liberty (that is, the reputation rights of a business or an individual). Evidence should indicate that there are no time, place or manner restrictions involved in the situation.

In any sign litigation, the attorney handles the pleadings and the persuasion, but must rely upon the sign user or manufacturer to provide the evidence that must be produced in court. Because this critical factor was not understood in some earlier cases, certain judicial decisions were made which were unnecessarily detrimental to signage. Apparently the sign users did not provide their attorneys with the evidence necessary to prove the value of the sign "by a preponderance of the evidence."

In preparation for litigation, either to protect a sign code or to overturn the sign code, it is important to understand that the burden of proof shifts depending on the nature of the litigation and the property interest you are seeking to regulate or protect.

As the area of law shifts in attempting to overturn a code that restricts commercial free speech, a substantial burden of proof falls on the person seeking to overturn the code. In the area of political speech, the burden of proof is nearly opposite. This must be understood early in the case, and the necessary experts must be available to testify. Without such testimony, a just cause may be lost. Such a loss is a tragedy not only to the immediate litigants, but also to those who follow. When legal precedent is set, it is extremely difficult to reverse the trend and requires much more substantial (and expensive) forms of evidenciary proof. This affects all sign users and manufacturers.

The sign industry faces two obstacles in any regulation challenge: 1) Does the substantive law favor you; and 2) what burden of proof do you have to get that the substantive law, whether judicial or legislative, favors you. Most often the sign companies understand that there is some form of legal precedent that favors them. Only the outdoor advertising industry seems to understand the importance of hard evidence in litigation. In certain cases such as *Eller v. City of Denver*, the evidence presented artfully won the case over the negative precedent of unfavorable earlier decisions. (*Art Neon* had preceded *Eller Outdoor*. Eller's attorneys had to overcome the negative precedent in *Art Neon*.)

At the low end of the use of police powers, the sign user carries a much heavier burden of proof. The state can virtually make any assertions, true or not, and stand by them. These assertions must then be refuted with research that is valid and accurate.

Preparing To Challenge A Code

Before anyone begins litigation, he needs to spend a considerable amount of time in consultation with the proper legal authorities to find out what burden of proof he is going to have to carry, how expensive it is going to be to do the necessary research and/or to hire the expert witnesses necessary to supply the research. Figure 10 provides a checklist of the two major areas that must be thoroughly explored before commencing any litigation with a municipality over a sign code.

FIGURE 10
Litigation Preparation Checklist

1. Legal Consultation
(a) Determine your burden of proof.
(b) Determine what type of evidence is required.
(c) Determine the litigation strategy.
(d) Establish a budget.

2. Expert Consultation
(a) Determine what documents and data are available.
(b) Determine what experts are available.
(c) Find out how to collect data which will stand up in court.
(d) Determine what expert testimony will cost.

It is important to remember that for anyone carrying the burden of proof, the court will not accept all people as expert witnesses on the subject. You may know as much about the economic value and contribution of a sign as a designated appraiser, but your testimony is not going to be accepted. These things must be carefully kept in mind because regardless of how right and correct your cause of action, if it is not implemented properly, you will lose.

**STREET SIGNAGE AND BUSINESS NET WORTH ANALYSIS:
AN INDUSTRY CASE STUDY**

INTRODUCTION

Signs can be analyzed as one of the rights assumed with the ownership of real property. In eminent domain law and in the majority of federal laws requiring compensation (such as the Uniform Relocation Assistance and Real Property Acquisition Act of 1970 (42 U.S.C. Section 4601 et seq.), the 1965 Highway Beautification Act (23 U.S.C. Section 131) and even the Fifth Amendment of the US Constitution), on-premise signs have consistently been difficult to fit into the ambit of compensation. Most studies of signs investigated them as part of a business strategy instead of as an inherently valuable part of the realty. In certain cases, however, signs were considered as real property. (*Metromedia, Inc. v. San Diego*, 453 U.S. 490, 101 S.Ct. 2882 (1981), on remand 32 Cal. 3d 180, 185 Cal. Rptr. 260, 649 P.2d 902 (1982).)

Signs with a land-use designation will substantially increase the value of the real estate. As an accessory or incidental use, they are made a part of the main designation of permissible uses. Normally, the damages from the loss of such signs must be quantified to be compensated.

Alexander Anolik, one of the leading experts in the travel agency industry, who is both a broker and an appraiser of business opportunities, related that he would not buy a travel agency without a sign. This statement added a dimension that helped reconcile the appraisal approaches to the value of the sign. A leading expert on travel agencies, recognized by the industry and the courts, equated the sign with the business and said they should not be separated.

(Signage is often dealt with ubiquitously. For instance, an outdoor advertising company's signs and structures are absolutely real property. But when an advertising agency rents the signs, they function the same as a television station. Particular items revert to personal property; they are not an appurtenance or a fixture to the land, and they are temporary by nature. This introduces certain problems in dealing with signs because, by their nature, they are somewhat elusive in legal definition, which has been reflected in the court's treatment of signs.)

Pricing and Profitability of Travel Agencies

According to the experts, 10% of the gross yearly volume of a travel agency is the maximum sales price of the agency, and 1% of the gross can be expected as profit. These figures will be modified by factors such as location, management and client and employee loyalty. If an agency were grossing $500,000, that agency could be purchased for $50,000 and expect $5000 profit on the annual gross revenues. To understand the worth of the sign, it should be measured against the net worth of the business.

(One Portland, OR, travel agency initially had no street exposure. At that point, with a rather low volume, it had a fifty-fifty ratio of leisure or pleasure versus commercial or business. Upon moving to a corner location, not ideal for street signage but about as good as could be found in the area, and building signs that had high visibility, legibility and readability, its mix was shifted to 80% leisure, pleasure oriented and 20% business or commercial. Effective signage can shift internal demands. This conclusion was pointed out earlier by Ray Anderson of 3M National Research Division: "Effective signage can shift the mix of customers.")

As the volume of the travel agency increases, it is expected that the net profit would gradually increase to 2%. This is dependent upon the nature of the clientele and the nature of the business.

*The charts and a great deal of the research material
for this article was compiled by Susan Claus.*

Signs as a Marketing Aid to a Particular Business

Most of the earlier literature deals with signs in terms of marketing research. Some of the writers' earlier works, as well as work done by other authorities, were essentially evaluation studies to determine the benefit of a sign to a particular business. (For information on such research see the **Small Business Marketing Aid 161**, by the same authors, copies of which are obtainable through Signs of the Times Publishing Company, Cincinnati, OH 45202.) That may cause some limited confusion to the value question because it concentrates on signage not as real property but as an adjunct to marketing. Such studies established the importance of a sign to a business that is highly impulse-oriented and consequently requires constant advertising to attract customers.

If similar items are sold on a large enough scale by a collection of stores or even by one large store, grossing $2 million a month, it becomes easy to fund alternate forms of advertising. For instance, a 7-Eleven store in the Portland, OR area has an average sales volume of about a $1 million per year with a net profit (before taxes and after wages and salaries are paid) of about $40,000. The franchisee or store operator rebates the parent company for all of the major media advertising. An entirely different media mix can be afforded by such a store when part of a chain.

THE LEISURE/PLEASURE-ORIENTED TRAVEL AGENCY STUDY

The initial property analysis which led to the present study was a non-existent, on-premise sign approximately 20 sq. ft., utilizing 6-in. black, acrylic letters affixed to the face of a one-story, six-unit commercial office building in the city of San Ramon, CA. The right to communicate to the public with this sign was part of the lease agreement. The city agreed that the sign was real estate and regulated under the related sign code as an appurtenance and accessory use to the property.

The business was part of a cluster of businesses with frontage on a collector street with an Average Daily Traffic (ADT) count of at least 18,700. (Combined weekly, two-directional, 24 hours, as of January 1985. The San Ramon traffic engineer recommended a five percent increase to update that figure for 1987.)

This study was conducted from the summer of 1986 to the Fall of 1987.

Limiting Conditions

There are a number of limiting conditions in using this report, but there are clear indications that it could be used to establish value for a retail business that did not have signage or has lost signage. To maintain the compensation value to the real property, it must be proven that the category of users cannot be replaced with another category of users who do not require signage.

The subject is located in California in a low-density suburban environment. California tends to be automobile oriented in shopping habits, somewhat typical of the rest of the US with the isolated exception of New York City.

The conclusions of this study are limited to property with a total lease area between 10,000 and 40,000 gross sq. ft. of property. These results may not be dependable for a larger property because alternate business strategies such as marketing and an on-premise sign with anchor tenants could overcome the loss of street communication.

Working in an environment such as California, where there is a large affluent population with a high disposable income, is also a factor in extending this evaluation to other areas. This study does not deal with a low-end market where there is limited discretionary income.

▶

Opposite Page

The leisure-oriented travel agency is a very specific destination-oriented business in which a sign is extremely important.

Businesses can be classified under two categories by consumer mind set: "destination-oriented" and "impulse-oriented." In the pure destination orientation, there is a demand for a specific product and/or specific customer loyalty. The prime example is a lawyer or an expensive restaurant. In either case, the prices for the service and the demand are instant-specific to such a group or can be so restricted by price that impulse-oriented street advertising is not apt to have a drastic effect on the overall demand. Consumption of these types of services is based on a conscious and deliberate choice. An example of an impulse-orientation is gasoline retailing or fast-food restaurants where sales are dependent on the flow of traffic in front of the business.

A leisure-oriented travel business cannot exist without drawing in the single-time customer who may travel only once or twice a year. Without constant advertising in front of the business in the form of a sign, these consumers will not be drawn in from the street.

Trade Area

Denny's restaurants are one example of a business that does a trade area survey to determine the potential customer breakdown. If a profile of the trade area is available which includes the density, types of occupation, income, employment level, housing, etc., the National Restaurant Assn. can give the basic number of meals that will be served in the area. The number of meals that will be consumed in a particular trade area is a derived demand. This is also true of items such as clothing and gasoline. Most consumer goods are derived demands.

Denny's has always done careful locational marketing. It does a trade area survey and counts the number of restaurants in the area to determine whether, based on gross profit per meal, a new restaurant could cover its fixed and variable costs. Signage is then able to draw in the impulse-oriented consumer in the "trade area" and add profit to the retail mix.

Shopping Centers and Impulse Buying

Typically, malls will have 50 to 60 stores and range between 500,000 and two million shoppers per month. Burbank Mall has monthly shopper traffic averaging 586,225 with 66 stores. Huntington Center, in Huntington Beach, CA has 1.875 million with 57 stores. Lakewood Center, with 250 stores, claims about 2.8 million shoppers per month. The malls with large, popular anchor stores typically draw the most traffic. If a retail business locates in a mall, the anchor stores draw in enough monthly exposures to offset the loss of vehicular traffic. (These figures for several southern California malls are simply a reference point. These figures are also typical of northern California.)

A shopping center with a marketing strategy that uses newspaper, television and other forms of advertisement to draw people to the shopping center itself, creates a similar situation as is present on the street. Impulse goods can be moved by motivating people to come to a particular location with various forms of advertising. When they are at the location, point-of-purchase advertising displays and even the signage on the front of a store can be used to influence the buyer.

Developing an Impulse- or Destination-Oriented Business

The sign on the street becomes profit-generating advertising. In addition to developing customer loyalty and repeat business, it signals to the impulse buyer who passes by on the street. The product in one case may have a destination orientation based on customer loyalty, and at the same time appeal to an impulse buyer. This adds to the sophistication of sign usage. The consumption habits of a consumer are a function of his income level. If there was no discretionary income above the basic necessities of life, one could not develop an impulse- or leisure-oriented travel business in the area, regardless of a sign's effectiveness.

Optimum Trade Area for Leisure-Oriented Travel Agency

For retail activity, leisure-oriented travel agencies are dependent upon the impulse consumer. The retail trade estimates that 65% of buying decisions are made once the customer enters the store. (J.C. Penney Co. Department Stores, "Visual Merchandising Reference," #701, June 1986.) Instead of being a predetermined destination, the travel agency will be a side-stop from an origin-destination path. The leisure-oriented travel agency, therefore, must be accessible and visible to its potential clients. (Annin, Karen J., "Looking Through the Glass to Effective Window Displays," Institute of Certified Travel Agencies, p. 3, November 1986.)

Location of a leisure-oriented travel agency differs from that of one whose clientele is primarily commercial or business related. (Anolik, Sorensen, **Evaluating a Travel Agency: Preventative Legal Care for Travel Agents**, p. 5, 1986.) The clientele of a leisure-oriented travel agency reflects the segment of the market that has the level of discretionary income necessary to afford the services offered. Besides locating within a trade area that has a high percentage of middle to upper income consumers, maintaining the image of the travel agency is a factor in its placement. The area should reflect the professionalism of the business.

The San Ramon Trade Area

The San Ramon Valley is a growing area based on non-defense industries and businesses such as food distribution, transportation, petro-chemicals and finance. The growth rate has ranged from 16-25% per year since 1975. (Valley Chamber of Commerce Demographics 1985-86.)

The residents in the San Ramon Valley are characterized as upwardly mobile and leisure-oriented with the kind of discretionary income that allows them to be active consumers. Retail trade makes up over 18% of the industry in San Ramon with financial/insurance/real estate being the second largest with 11.8%. (Valley Chamber of Commerce Demographics 1985-86.) This retail orientation indicates the probability of survival for such a retail activity as a leisure-oriented travel agency.

Trade Area Analysis

A total trade area analysis was completed for this evaluation. Of the 18 other travel agencies located in the San Ramon Valley trade area, eight were located in the city of San Ramon itself. Based on the income level of the potential consumers within the trade area, it was possible to calculate the potential volume of travel sales. By comparing the potential sales volume figure with the number of travel agencies, the probability for the success of a travel agency in the area was derived. If the probability for success could not be demonstrated, the effectiveness of such a study would be minimized regardless of the availability of signage. It was determined that the San Ramon Valley trade area should be able to adequately support the subject business as well as the other agencies in the area.

In light of these calculations, and based on past sales and industry projections, the business owner projected certain revenue targets. While the other agencies in the area seemed to be drawing sufficient sales volume, the subject was not meeting its projected revenue targets.

The projections were felt to be reasonable. The other travel agencies were surveyed by an expert, and they were all doing similar volume given locational factors. This was the business owner's second travel agency. The traffic count, trade area and type of consumers were comparable to his other location. There was no reason the subject business should not perform as well. The one outstanding difference is that the other location had a sign of at least 40 sq. ft. advertising the business. Its visibility, an external obsolescence factor, was far less than what it would have been on this site, given the size of the sign. A survey of travel agency clients showed that about 70% were repeat users of services and that about 35% drove by the business they selected to use at least once a month, 15% at least daily. That would indicate that of the traffic drawn in by a sign, 70% would do business again. The 35% who frequently drove by the agencies are those who would be reminded by a sign of the services available at that location.

143

APPLICATION OF THE THREE APPROACHES

The analyses with the three approaches, income (or loss of income) discounted cash flow method, market approach (competitive market lease approach) and the cost of replacement with alternate advertising, indicated that the numbers on the first two approaches nearly parallel the purchase price of the business. These conclusions support the methods of approaching value which were used in this evaluation.

Income (or Loss of Income) Discounted Cash Flow Approach

To understand the significance of having exposure to the street frontage in order to advertise a business, the writers compiled a set of figures gathered from travel agencies and experts in the field. Table 10 has a set of income figures based over five years, discounting the income to its net present value. Net present value in this case means the difference, if any, between the present value of expected benefits or positive cash flow and the present value of capital outlay or negative cash flow. (American Institute of Real Estate Appraisers, **The Dictionary of Real Estate Appraisal**, 211 (1984).)

TABLE 10

The discounted cash flow analysis demonstrates the difference of the net present value of the cash flows before taxes, with and without signage. An inherent assumption for demonstration purposes is that the business will lose money for the first year. The second year, the income nets $35,000. The third, fourth and fifth years, the business income will level at $50,000 yearly net. A 30% factor as lost net income revenue from lost signage is used. Most agency owners and experts believe from 25% to 40% is the minimum that a business generates from a sign.

Considering future cash flow, the figures would determine what the future benefits would bring if the business was placed for sale in the marketplace. The expected net cash flow should always be much higher than the actual price at which the business would be sold to a knowledgeable purchaser.

TABLE 10
San Ramon Area Travel Agency
Discounted Cash Flow Analysis
5 Year Projection
With Signage — Without Signage
30% Decrease Without Signage

Description	Start-up Costs	Year 1	Year 2	Year 3	Year 4	Year 5
Net income with signage	($11,000)	($8,000)	$35,000	$50,000	$50,000	$50,000
Net income 30% without signage	($11,000)	($10,400)	$24,500	$35,000	$35,000	$35,000

	Varying Capital Risk Interest Rates			
	5%	10%	15%	20%
Net present value of cash flow with signage	$136,663	$113,415	$94,831	$79,781
Net present value of cash flow without signage 30%	$ 87,770	$ 71,727	$58,908	$48,546
Net difference of cash flow in dollars	$ 48,893	$ 41,688	$35,923	$31,235
Net difference of cash flow by percentage of cash	35.8%	36.8%	37.9%	39.2%

Source: Signs of the Times magazine, May, 1987.

Competitive Market Lease Approach

A matched pair study and interviews with several real estate leasing experts paralleled the remarks of Anolik. Two of the agents stated that while there may be a certain amount of saving in the lease, the probability of failure increases so much that the business becomes difficult to sell. They recommended against even leasing to tenants in retail-oriented business without street exposure signage.

TABLE 11

**San Ramon Valley Leased Office Space Prices
Broken Down By Price Per Square Foot
Value For Street Frontage Vs. Non-Street Frontage**

Item	Subject	Leased Space Comp #1	Leased Space Comp #2	Leased Space Comp #3	Leased Space Comp #4
Leased sq. ft.	1500	1500	1500	1500	1500
Price/sq. ft. —					
Street frontage	$2.00	$2.00	$1.65	$1.25	$2.00
Non St. frontage	$1.25	$1.25	$1.40	$0.90	$1.45
Price/sq. ft. diff.	$0.75	$0.75	$0.25	$0.35	$0.55
% Price/sq. diff.	37.50%	37.50%	15.15%	28.00%	27.50%
Price/sq. ft. diff. multiply by sq. ft.	$1125 = Difference in lease dollars per month				
Lease $ per month annualized	$13,500				

$13,500 is annualized from the $1125 net monthly lease difference. The net lease of $13,500 yearly as an income stream is calculated with varying interest rates over one-to-20-year periods to obtain the present value of the income stream, or the present worth today of that income stream over the period of its lease.

Lease Period In Years	Varying Risk Capital Interest Rates				
	5.0%	10.0%	12.0%	15.0%	20.0%
	Present Values Per Year				
1	$ 12,857	$ 12,273	$ 12,054	$ 11,739	$ 11,250
2	$ 25,102	$ 23,430	$ 22,816	$21,947	$20,625
3	$ 36,764	$ 33,573	$ 32,425	$30,824	$28,438
4	$ 47,870	$ 42,793	$ 41,004	$38,542	$34,948
5	$ 58,448	$ 51,176	$ 48,664	$45,254	$40,373
6	$ 68,522	$ 58,796	$ 55,504	$51,091	$44,894
7	$ 78,116	$ 65,724	$ 61,611	$56,166	$48,662
8	$ 87,253	$ 72,022	$ 67,063	$60,579	$51,802
9	$ 95,956	$ 77,747	$ 71,931	$64,416	$54,418
10	$104,243	$ 82,952	$ 76,278	$67,753	$56,598
11	$112,137	$ 87,683	$ 80,159	$70,655	$58,415
12	$119,654	$ 91,985	$ 83,624	$73,178	$59,929
13	$126,813	$ 95,895	$ 86,718	$75,372	$61,191
14	$133,632	$ 99,450	$ 89,480	$77,280	$62,243
15	$140,125	$102,682	$ 91,947	$78,939	$63,119
16	$146,310	$105,620	$ 94,149	$80,382	$63,849
17	$152,200	$108,291	$ 96,115	$81,637	$64,458
18	$157,809	$110,719	$ 97,871	$82,728	$64,965
19	$163,152	$112,926	$ 99,438	$83,676	$65,387
20	$168,240	$114,933	$100,837	$84,501	$65,739

Source: Signs of the Times magazine, May, 1987.

Values for the subject property are based on correlation features between the subject and comparables. The graph is simplified for demonstration purposes. Comparable #1 is judged to be the best comparable as it is across the street and within a couple of blocks from the subject property and thus a direct competitor for lease space. The other three comparables have variations in percentage differences of price-per-square-foot frontage due to effective ages of the buildings, two story versus one story, street location, etc. All comparables demonstrate the importance of price difference due to street frontage and non-street frontage. The savings of forfeiting exposure does not make up the revenue lost by not having a sign.

Cost of Replacement

Since the sign could not be replaced with another sign, the cost of building another sign became irrelevant. It was necessary to find alternate forms of visual communication to replace it. Advertising data was researched and compiled to replace the typical exposures on the street with alternate forms of advertising. Those figures approximated $160,704 annually. (See Table 12.) This figure might be lowered, but if eight typical retail businesses under one roof combined their advertising budgets, they could afford this mix of advertising.

TABLE 12
Cost of Replacement

Variables to Calculate DAILY EFFECTIVE CIRCULATION (DEC) — Annualized	
# Cars per day/direction	9,350
# of directions	2
Passenger factor per car	1.60
# of days in a year	365

Formula:

9,350	X	2	=	18,700	Cars per day/direction
18,700	X	1.60	=	29,920	Daily effective circulation
29,920	X	365	=	10,920,800	Daily effective circulation — annualized

Cost to Obtain Same Number of Exposures Over a One-Year Period

Media	Cost	Number of Impressions
Local newspaper A	$ 37,606	5,267,404
Local newspaper B	$ 4,700	556,344
Local radio station	$ 43,518	3,159,096
Metro area newspaper A	$ 34,900	1,181,952
Metro area newspaper B	$ 8,650	366,598
Metro area newspaper C	$ 5,870	121,475
Off beat newspaper A	$ 8,960	231,131
	$144,204	10,920,000
Cost per impression		$0.013

Production

Eight radio commercials	$ 7,000
Six newspaper advertisements	$ 8,000
One magazine advertisement	$ 1,500
Total media and production costs	$160,704

Estimated cost to replace exposures from lost signage	$ 160,704

Source: Signs of the Times magazine, May, 1987.

On a two-directional street, as in the case of the travel agency, the number of cars per day per direction per traffic survey is multiplied by the number of directions to give a total count of cars per day. A multiplier or "passenger factor" generated from the local city transportation engineers is multiplied to the number of cars per day to get a "daily effective circulation" (DEC). The DEC is then annualized for a yearly number of exposures generated from the on-premise sign.

Both media and production costs are added together for a total cost to replace exposures from lost signage. The proposed media schedule included six different 30-column-inch newspaper ads, eight radio commercials and a magazine ad. For a small business, such an advertising campaign is not financially feasible.

Land Valuation Capitalization Method

A recent sale for a shopping center was found in the area. It was located on a site of 119,525 sq. ft. The rentable retail space was 33,905 sq. ft. The total net monthly (with the tenants paying taxes and maintenance charges) was $40,000. The center sold for $5.3 million. The capitalization on the annualized net monthly income at the purchase price would be:

$$\frac{\$40,000 \times 12}{\$5,300,000} = .09 \text{ (Cap Rate)}$$

The selling agent said that if the center did not have street frontage, the rent would fall to around $1.00/ sq.ft. versus the current $1.25, which is a 20% decline. That 20% decline applied to the annualized income results in a property value decline. The lowered property value would be:

$$\frac{(\$40,000 \times 12)^* \ 80\%}{.09 \text{ (Cap Rate)}} = \$4,266.667$$

This property value decline from reduced lease income due to loss of street frontage is calculated:

Property value with street frontage	— $5,300,000
Property value without street frontage	— $4,266,667
Loss in value due to loss in signage	— $1,033,333

With the current capitalization rate, the entire property's value would be diminished by approximately 20% with the loss of street frontage. (There should not be too much reliance on this since it is just one sale of a center where contract rents may be below market rents. The capitalization rate method itself is what is significant.) This result is not inconsistent with other analyses used in this paper.

(The topic of this paper is of special significance to urban planners. The existence of any main street or downtown shopping center is threatened if the right of exposure to traffic is severely restricted. According to Robert Sprague, managing partner of Retail Consultant Services in New Hampshire, the downtown portion of the national retail market has dropped from 97% to 15% since 1958. The radical decline of Portland, OR's central business district is typical; a 1986 study for the Portland Development Commission reports that while the central business district's share of the retail sales of the metropolitan area dropped from 17% to 4% since 1958, over nine million square feet of leasable store space was constructed in major shopping centers. Nationally, there are over 28,500 shopping centers with 3.7 billion square feet of leasable space according to John Chapman, research director for the International Council of Shopping Centers.)

All retailers are competing for the same dollar. A shopping center will destroy a competitive district if that district does not have the tools to compete. (See "Medford merchant resists the exodus," *The Oregonian*, August 30, 1987.)

RECONCILIATION OF VALUE

In order to reconcile the three approaches to value, one must choose which approach or set of approaches to give the most weight and explain why. As the value of the rights for visual communication to the street has been established, the cost of replacing those with some alternate media mix has usually been rejected. This analysis may explain why and how the cost of replacement has not previously been feasible and how it might be successful in the future.

In the market approach in this case, the analysis was simply comparing the leases and concluding that approximately $.75 per sq. ft. per month would have been saved by the lessee by renting space that had no visual communication rights to the street. The discounted cash flow approach shows a figure that is somewhat similar. The cost of replacement through other media gives a much higher figure for the losses. For the value of this business' rights to communicate with the collector street, the writers chose to reject the cost of replacement approach and to utilize an approach that is between the market data sales approach, which is the cost of alternate lease, and the discounted cash flow approach.

The loss to the subject, as one of several tenants of similar square footage, must be considered in light of the loss of value to the entire parcel of ground. Thus, the loss must be multiplied by the number of tenants to determine the loss to the entire property. Any tenant considering this will be disinclined to lease unless the rent is lowered substantially to reflect the decreased property value.

The best way to understand the full loss to the value of the property is to look at what it would cost to place all of the advertisements for that property in a competitive media mix. That would suffice for all of the tenants if they chain-advertised for that piece of property. Although the cost approach is inadequate for one business, it may very accurately reflect the loss of value to the entire piece of property. Figure 11 is a summary of the conclusions of the analyses:

FIGURE 11
Travel Agency with $500,000 Gross Sales Commission Revenues

Net present worth of business	$50,000	Purchase price
1) Discounted cash flow gross revenue for operations loss 30%	$41,466	Net present value 5 years, 10% discount note
2) Lease costs of $.75 per month per square foot less for non-signage street location	$51,176	Net present value 5 years, 10% discount note
3) Cost of replacement with alternate forms of commercial communication	$160,704	Annual expense

Obsolescence

Internal functional and external obsolescence are important factors in appraising. The value of a sign is ideal to illustrate this. Certain parts of the functional obsolescence, namely design, may be curable. Under certain circumstances, it may be incurable if it is built into a company logo that cannot be corrected. Also, a certain letter size is needed to communicate from a particular distance, and certain requirements need to be met for visibility. All of the obsolescence factors can be related.

Factors such as the speed of traffic, width of the street, items in front of the street, and landscaping offer measurement scales which were worked out for this evaluation.

CONCLUSIONS

The preliminary conclusions of this study are: 1) the net worth of businesses can be nearly destroyed by the loss of street signage; 2) property values in the area could be affected by as much as 25%; and 3) certain kinds of businesses could lose an opportunity to function because the cost of replacing lost signage street exposure is totally cost prohibitive.

Another possible corollary is that an aggressive municipal anti-sign code makes a statement about the type of businesses the town encourages. It limits the pattern of ownership for the real estate in the town. The small real estate will be at such a disadvantage that investment capital would go to other areas. This area needs much additional study, but it further indicates the value of visual communication rights and their significance in a community where they are inappropriately applied.

In the manner that the lessor took away the right of the lessee to communicate with the thoroughfare, there is an absolute diminution of value to the realty. Any lessor or property owner who does not aid a small business owner to obtain all possible visual communication rights to the local public vehicular streets works against his own real property interest. Without street signage, the mix of potential businesses to lease is lowered, and the amount of rent the tenant can afford to pay is diminished.

One leasing agent stated that he has leased to people "who so desperately wanted to get into business that they would take any space. These businesses have a higher probability of business failure than those which understand the necessity of obtaining a sign."

A small retail center cannot survive against larger centers that have anchor tenants, media advertising campaigns and a carefully selected identification program unless the smaller center has signage on the public street. One real estate broker recommends not even building such a center without signage, given the high price of land in the area.

Finally, the 25% to 40% of sales commission revenue generated from a sign is the significant difference between survival and failure for a retail store.

HANDICAPPED SIGNAGE

Along with the need for quality design and construction, the sign specifier should be aware of another need — the need to make public use buildings accessible to the handicapped. This is an important subject that is both complicated and easy to understand. It is complicated because of the maze of statistics, documents, government agencies and private interests involved in the formulation of the Uniform Federal Accessibility Standards (UFAS). It is relatively easy to understand because the intent of the standards is laudable, and the actual proposed minimum guideline standards are quite basic.

Introduction

The Uniform Federal Accessibility Standards document — published in 1984 — embodies an agreement to minimize the differences between four federal agencies which are authorized to issue standards under the Architectural Barriers Act of 1968. These four agencies are: the General Services Administration, the Department of Housing and Urban Development, the Department of Defense and the US Postal Service. To ensure compliance with the standards, Congress established the Architectural and Transportation Barriers Compliance Board (ATBCB), which is comprised of members representing 11 federal agencies. According to a UFAS document, it was the intent of the four standard-setting agencies to comply not only with the guidelines adopted by the ATBCB, but also those published by the American National Standards Institute (ANSI).

ANSI is a non-governmental national association which publishes a wide variety of recommended engineering and design standards — from the width of screw threads to lumber specifications. ANSI standards for barrier-free design were originally developed by a committee of 52 organizations representing handicapped people, rehabilitation professionals, designers, builders and manufacturers. The resulting standards of ANSI A117.1 are titled "Specifications for Making Buildings and Facilities Accessible to and Usable by Physically Handicapped People."

It is important to note that the ANSI standards have generally been accepted by both the public and private sectors. Indeed, with some amendments, the UFAS document follows ANSI A117.1 in format.

Standard Procedures

As pertaining to the sign industry, the Minimum Guidelines and Requirements for Accessible Design (MGRAD) are primarily covered under section 4.30 of the UFAS document. The 1984 version of UFAS lists information on character proportion, color contrast, raised or indented characters, symbols of accessibility, mounting location and mounting height.

In another section of UFAS, there are provisions for raised characters in elevators and tactile warnings at stairs and on doors leading to hazardous areas.

In general, the UFAS document closely parallels the 1986 ANSI A117.1 standards. Both documents agree that characters and symbols shall contrast with their background — either light characters on a dark background or dark characters on a light background. Both documents agree on character proportion, i.e., letters and numbers on signs shall have a width-to-height ratio of between 3:5 and 1:1 and a stroke width-to-height ratio of between 1:5 and 1:10 — utilizing an upper case "X" for measurement. Finally, both documents agree on the size, location and use of the International Symbol of Accessibility.

There are, however, differences between the documents. And it is those differences which have ultimately fostered much debate and expensive, time-consuming research. For example: the 1984 UFAS document specifies that characters or symbols should be raised or incised (indented) 1/32 of an inch. The 1986 ANSI standards only recommend that tactile symbols be raised. In addition, the ANSI standards also advise the use of a sans serif typeface — a typeface not in the UFAS document. Also, the UFAS document is specific about mounting location and height for accessible signs.

These issues are further complicated by the Architectural Transportation and Barriers Compliance Board's most recent attempt to rectify these discrepancies in its "proposed rules," published in September of 1987 under the heading: "Minimum Guidelines and Requirements for Accessible Design" (MGRAD). Once again, the idea behind this latest look at the sign standards is commendable. Unfortunately, the MGRAD document tends to only confuse the issue. As reported in the September 16 *Federal Register:*

> Recognizing the widespread application of the ANSI standard and the desirability of uniformity, the ATBCB in MGRAD included provisions that were consistent with the technical specifications of ANSI A117.1-1980 wherever it was deemed appropriate.
>
> In reviewing the ANSI technical requirements during MGRAD development, however, the ATBCB found that in some cases, with regard to some subjects, there was not sufficient research and/or field experience to support a federal requirement at the time. Those provisions were reserved in MGRAD. The reserved provisions include...all provisions dealing with signage.

In other words...back to the drawing board. To verify or debunk the ANSI sign standards, the ATBCB funded two research projects: one specifically on signage, and the second on signage and other informational systems for low-vision persons.

Essentially, the results of this research upheld two 1986 ANSI standards. It 1) established the upper case letter "X" as a standard measurement for determining character proportion; and 2) prohibited incised letters.

Furthermore, it was found that "there was not sufficient justification to make an MGRAD change for the uniform character proportion ratios on signs as specified jointly by ANSI and UFAS."

All told, the ATBCB's proposed rules virtually encompass all 1986 ANSI sign standards with the one addition of the UFAS 54-66-in. tactile sign mounting recommendation on the latch side of the door. The MGRAD's proposed rules also note one exception: "The provisions of ANSI 4.28.4 are not mandatory for temporary information on room and space signage such as currrent occupant's name, provided the permanent room or space identification complies with ANSI 4.30."

What It All Means
All of this confusion and complication, it should be mentioned, is exacerbated by the fact that as of late 1987, these standards are only the proposed rules for MGRAD. The actual "law" is still to be established some time in the future. However, there are several strong indications of what a sign specifier should probably do to comply with the probable standards:

1) When signing a building to be accessible to the handicapped, use raised (1/32) letters versus incised letters (even though the UFAS document presently allows for both). It appears highly likely that only raised letters will be allowed in the new code.

2) Letters and symbols should contrast — but don't fall into the trap of believing that the ultimate code will allow both light characters on dark and dark on light. Why? Because an ANSI advisory appendix states that the greatest readability usually is achieved with light characters on a dark background. To be safe, it is probably better to follow what ANSI advises — it may become the law.

3) A sans serif typeface "without excess flourishes" is preferred by ANSI.

4) Although not presently specified by ANSI, it would be wise to mount and locate all signs which conform to the UFAS document 54-66 in. above the floor on the latch. This is recommended in MGRAD. Also, it is advisable to place signs within 30 degrees to the center line of the handicapped person's eyes. Many people with disabilities, states the ATBCB, have limitations in the movement of their heads.

5) In building complexes where finding locations independently may be a necessity (ex. college compuses), the use of tactile maps is recommended by the ANSI to help the visually impaired.

6) Additional — or secondary — visual cues, such as wall murals and bright color patterns are recommended.

7) Familiarize yourself with the proper use and placement of the International Symbol of Accessibility.

8) These accessibility requirements should be specified for all new construction of public use buildings — not just federally funded buildings. This is because the ANSI standards are widely accepted by many state building codes.

Many existing public use buildings not in compliance with the standards should probably be "re-signed" to comply. At present, enforcement of these standards for existing buildings appears minimal, but that is no guarantee of what will be enforced in the future.

Handicapped signs are for both interior and exterior identifications. Photo courtesy of ASI Sign Systems, Marina del Rey, CA.

Access Information

The International Symbol of Accessibility was adopted in 1969 by Rehabilitation International at its 11th World Congress on "Rehabilitation of the Disabled." The symbol tells a handicapped individual that the building he is entering conforms (or in some cases, does not conform) to accessibility laws.

Design of the symbol must contain two elements: a wheelchair figure plus either a square border or background. If the wheelchair figure is white, the background figure should be blue. Conversely, if the border and wheelchair are blue, the background is white. No other design element should be introduced onto the sign except if the building in question is not accessible to the needs of the handicapped person. Then, a diagonal red slash across the wheelchair figure should always face right unless used with a directional sign indicating to the left. In addition, specifications concerning location, size and visibility are also recommended though not mandatory.

FIGURE 12
International Symbol of Accessibility

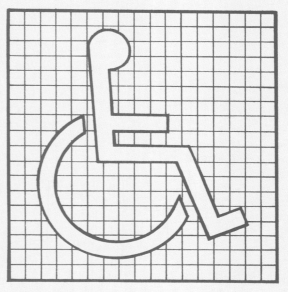

(a)   Proportions

(b)   Display Conditions

153

Figures

DATE DUE

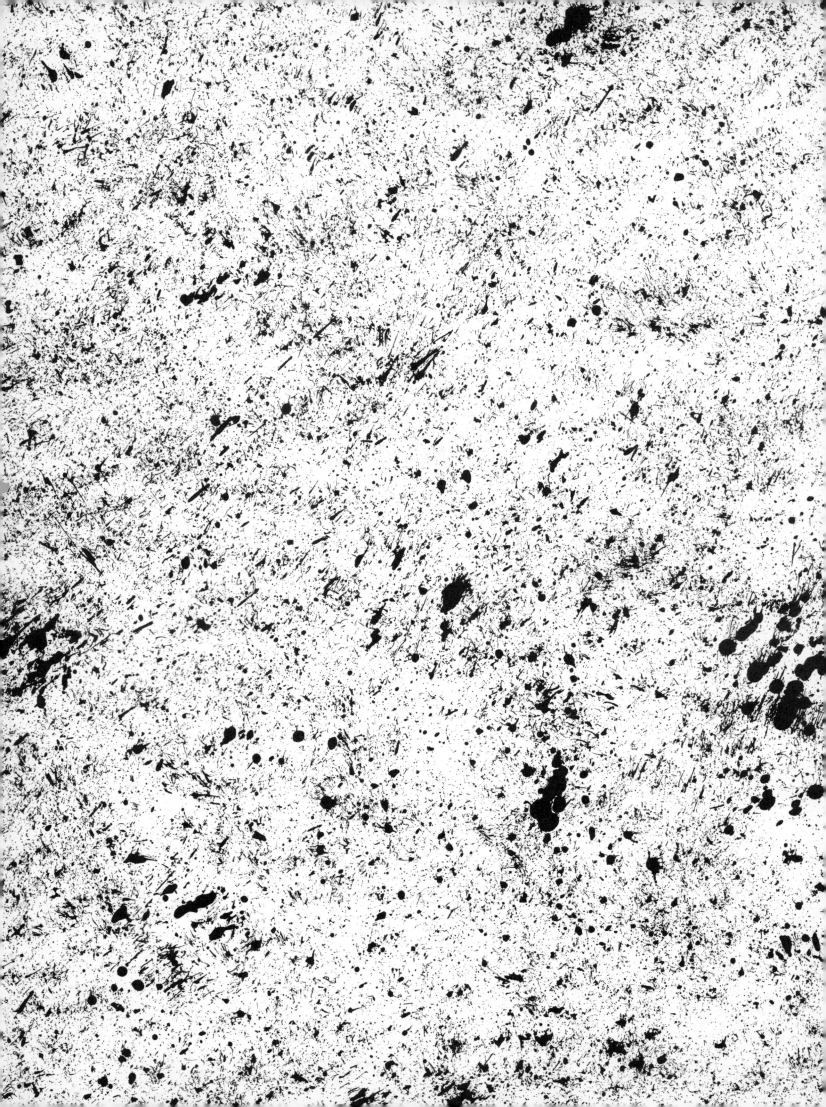